D1096971

Praise for Road to Awesome

Profound ideas and actionable practices to lead with clarity and intentionality!

Dr. Peppard's honesty and vulnerability combined with his message of positivity and hope make this an engaging and delightful read. *Road to Awesome* reveals how the work we do truly matters and Darrin provides inspiring ways to excel at organizational management as well as instructional leadership creating a culture and climate where everyone can succeed feeling seen, heard, valued, and trusted.

If you are ready to inject energy and joy into how you approach your work as a champion for everyone in your learning community, this is the book for you!

Lainie Rowell
Bestselling Author, Award-Winning Educator, TEDx Speaker

Wow! In this updated edition of *Road to Awesome,* Darrin practices what he preaches. He doesn't just accept what is already good, but he refines, reflects, and makes it even better. With a new focus on instructional leadership, balanced with personal and professional experiences, Darrin reminds us that *awesome* is a place we can all get to if we are willing to do the work. Darrin has done the work, and this book has me better equipped to do the work myself. The road less traveled is a scary place to be, but thanks to this powerful book, you don't have to travel it alone. Darrin is right there with you.

Dave Schmittou
Author, Coach, Consultant
Former Building and District Administrator

This book is a must-read if you believe a positive attitude is critical for students, staff, parents and leaders. Darrin's personal story and experiences, in addition to the personal stories of others, helps support and remind us of the need for a positive attitude and a positive mindset. One simply cannot excel in facing today's challenges without a game plan and strategies to lead with a positive attitude. This book provides the insights, motivation, and strategies for you to not only lead with a positive mindset and attitude it also helps you be your best so you can lead your best.

Randal Russell
Superintendent

Road to Awesome: The Journey of a Leader by Darrin Peppard is a personal and intimate account of his journey to finding his passion and purpose in life. The book emphasizes the importance of mentorship, offers a unique perspective on the evolving role of a school principal and challenges the reader to think differently about leadership, promoting an open, collaborative, and inclusive culture. Darrin's book focuses on clarity and intentionality in a leader's work and is not a traditional "how-to" guide; it encourages readers to be the game-changer. Highly recommended for those feeling lost, unmotivated, needing inspiration or a "Pep-talk" in their leadership journey.

Dr. Chad Lang
President – Recalibrate Educational Services LLC
2018 Missouri Athletic Director of the Year

The title *Road to Awesome* is an excellent description for what lies ahead in these pages. Darrin talks candidly about his leadership journey - the ups, the down, the highs, the lows, the moments of success, and the moments of deep questioning. He's been in our shoes, and he's experienced what it means to transition from from someone *working in the system* to someone with the responsibility to *work on the system*.

Darrin's message to live and lead with intentionality and clarity is food for our leadership souls. Many other messages resound throughout this book - the need to lead WITH others, be your authentic self, and learn from mistakes will all resonate with early career and veteran leaders alike.

Larry Dake
Assistant Superintendent

Darrin gifts us with the story of his personal journey to and through a career in public education. Easy to read and exuding humility, Darrin shares many poignant take-aways. I was struck by how consistently he credited the mentors in his life for putting him on his *road to awesome*. Your leadership moves will be clarified, reinforced and, at times, challenged by this great read! Darrin consistently reminds us to "focus on the things we can control, let go of the things we cannot, we rise by lifting others, and we change the world one conversation at time."

Eric Bolz
Vice President of Research and District Engagement for
The Center for Educational Effectiveness
Outliers in Education Podcast Co-Host

With experience as a school and district leader, Darrin's practical, human-centered approach provides essential tools leaders need to engage all staff in understanding how their personal contributions impact, first and foremost, the learners and also the system's health and success. *Road to Awesome* encourages us to be the champions of organizations by leading alongside our teams while also seeing it from the balcony as we all travel our own road to awesome!

Summer Stephens
2023 Nevada Superintendent of the Year

Darrin Peppard's story is one that almost every single teacher or school leader can relate to. He shows how being a school leader is no easy task. However, he provides insights, wisdom, and even strategies to help you lead from your heart in order to promote a positive culture for your entire organization. This book will make you laugh, cry, learn, and relate to Darrin as you enjoy this unforgettable road trip on the Road to Awesome.

Dr. Brandon Beck
Teacher, Speaker, Author, Coach

In this wonderful book, the author, Darrin Peppard, shares his journey in education as a teacher, coach, and administrator. He shares 6 essential keys to be an effective leader. These keys are shared through excellent examples and stories. You also will receive great ideas to implement to improve your school culture. This is a must read for all educators and I believe it can help any leader, whether you work in education or another industry!

Jim Johnson
Former Teacher, Coach, Speaker and Author

Darrin takes you on a journey that will impact any educator no matter your role or number of years of experience. His practical ideas, that you can implement almost immediately at your school, serve as a great resource for anyone looking to enhance and improve the culture and climate at your school. His book will leave you feeling inspired and give you a road map to help you be the champion of your school/organization. The journey on the road to awesome is one you don't want to miss! So, buckle up, and start your trip!

Melissa Wright
Educator, Author, Speaker
Jostens Renaissance Hall of Fame 2022

Road to Awesome is a masterclass of knowledge that provides pivotal concepts for aspiring and current educational leaders looking to improve their abilities and take their schools to awesome.

Jonathan Alsheimer
Teacher, Speaker, Author

The Road To Awesome is the road of discovery of oneself and discovering what one is capable of. Throughout his book, *Road To Awesome*, Darrin reminds us that, "We are in the people business, don't ever forget that." Everything we do in education and in life is about the people. The little people (kids) and the big people (adults). The Road To Awesome is about helping people to believe in themselves and making them feel valued in the process.

No matter if you are at the beginning of your journey, at the rest stop, or miles down the road, *Road To Awesome* is an awesome book to have in your glove box through your journey in life and education. Get out and get going on your Road To Awesome!

Santiago Meza
Elementary Administrator

One of the benefits of time is that it shows whether there's alignment between words and deeds with a leader. All it takes is one look at what Darrin has shared in this book and who he is to see that he's been consistent over the long haul. That stability of message, presence, and action is part of what builds confidence in people. I've seen over the years that every great leader was a great advocate of and for people. You can clearly see this advocacy of Darrin's in his commitment to culture, and that leads me to another salient point. Great leaders cultivate and nurture great cultures, and great cultures put people first. This is your opportunity to do just that with your life. Get this book and make this year your year of impact!

Vernon Wright
Speaker, Author, Consultant, Leader

Road to Awesome
The Journey of a Leader

Darrin Peppard EdD

Road to Awesome: The Journey of a Leader

To my amazing wife and incredible daughter.
You energize and motivate me; you inspire me, and I
love you both so very much.

In the span of 24 hours in late November 2020,
I lost my Oma and my former secretary
Marilyn Rosette. It was unbelievably difficult,
and I miss and cherish them both.

To the four of you: Jess, Liz, Oma, and Marilyn –
I dedicate this book to you.

Table of Contents

Foreward

By Bethany Hill

Instructional leadership is the goal of every school leader. It requires a high level of self-awareness, and the ability to read the climate and culture of an organization. Self-aware instructional leaders are process observers and mappers. They build their vision through understanding the culture, the people involved, and the various climates that impact the organization as a whole. To be a highly effective instructional leader, one must honor the existing terrain and map out different routes to achieve a common goal, all while keeping in mind each person involved. Honoring someone's journey is appreciating that one route cannot get everyone to the same destination.

A leadership journey is much like a highway. There are moments where the road is flat for miles with not a car in sight, and the air is crystal clear. During those long stretches of road, we can get comfortable and enjoy the surrounding view because we can see what is ahead and predict the terrain. The straight highway has no bumps, no traffic, nothing to slow us down. In fact, this may prompt us to speed up a little. We become confident and in a groove. Life is awesome and getting better every minute! We know where we are headed, and the destination is clear. Predictability and being in the moment makes us feel good, and it is easy. At some point, the road will change. Being prepared for the curves and turns ahead provides a plan for when to slow down, pump the brakes, and turn the wheel. If the driver isn't prepared for the change in terrain, they can lose sight of the road. The road to awesome will have some unknowns, and reminds us to expect the unexpected.

Just as the straight stretches of highway bring us comfort, we have straight stretches in life's journey where everything is running smoothly and efficiently. Goals are being met, items are being checked off the list, and our leadership is empowering to ourselves and others. What if life was one long stretch of highway? Where would that take us, and would we become better educators and better humans? Think about the times when you have learned important lessons. Was it when things were running like a well oiled machine, or was it during an engine failure with challenging circumstances? When the rubber hits the road, we learn more from the wrong turns, missed exits, and malfunctions. They make us uncomfortable, induce emotion, and force us to think of what went wrong.

The education profession is no straight stretch of highway. Detours will throw us off course, speed bumps will slow us down, and raging storms will stop us completely because we cannot see the road ahead. It is in those unsettled moments that we have to pull over, park, and think about the next action. That could be recalculating our internal GPS and establishing another way to get to where we are headed. It might be exhibiting patience by riding the storm out, waiting and reflecting before the next action. The pause can lead to new routes or the realization that we are lost and unsure if the destination is the best one. The journey on the Road to Awesome might lead us to a crossroads, where intuition is telling us to go one way, but the planned route tells us to go the other way. Sometimes, our gut tells us the right way to turn and opens up a new view with a clearer vision. The bumps, winding turns, and steep hills are what make us strong enough to be awesome.

Establishing a vision for awesomeness requires planning for a roadtrip with a team of people who see the same level of excellence and the leader knowing they cannot achieve excellence alone. Expect roadblocks, knowing they are only temporary stops on the Road to Awesome. We will not find perfection on this journey, but we can find excellence if we allow focus and dedication to do the driving.

Road to Awesome: The Journey of a Leader places the heart of Darrin Peppard on display and adds just the perfect touch of sincerity and clarity. He shares stories of leadership successes and failures that will speak to your mind, your commitment to the profession, and will remind you of your WHY. The Road to Awesome, in my mind, is infinite. We will never officially arrive, but the destinations along the way will leave us hungry to continue driving forward with purpose. That will ensure our vision for excellence is never ending. It will also ensure that we remember to never travel alone, because great leaders cannot safely function as a lone transient. The Road to Awesome should never be lonely and should allow others to pass up from time to time, taking turns and sharing in the navigation of awesomeness.

So open the door, take a seat, buckle up, and prepare to take off! The road to awesome awaits you! Remember to take some time to enjoy the drive.

Route 66 on the way to Oatman, AZ. This is just outside of Kingman, AZ where my teaching career began.

Introduction

"Two roads diverged in a wood, and I –
I took the one less traveled by,
And it has made all the difference."
~ Robert Frost

We all know this iconic phrase, the final lines from Robert Frost's poem *The Road Not Taken*. How many times in our own lives have we come to a moment where two roads diverged in front of us, and we had to make a decision? The core of this book is the story about a moment in my life when two roads diverged, and I had a choice to make. A choice that, upon reflection, changed me as an educator, a leader, a husband, a father, and a human being. This is the story about my life as a career educator, as a lover of education, of working with kids, of supporting and growing teachers and leaders. This is the story of someone who discovered a great truth and feels compelled to share it with anyone who will listen or read it.

When I wrote my first book, *Road to Awesome: Empower, Lead, Change the Game*, I was not sure what to do. How did I begin? What, exactly, should it look like? I only knew I wanted to write a book and get it published. I learned a great deal along the way, including what people really want to read in your book: your stories. I really thought I had to have some magic formula for my book to be good, for anyone to want to read it. The truth is, people want to learn from each other, have their ideas validated, and allow themselves to be curious. My friend and fellow educational author, Lainie Rowell, once told me of her writing process. She writes not to provide answers but to find answers. This might be the best statement I have ever heard and more true about writing than most people know. As I sit, writing this introduction, I am thinking deeply about how I have evolved and how education has changed since the release of the first book.

In my first book, I shared what I believed to be the six most important things in school leadership. Six things that were most important *to me* but were never meant to be sold as *your* most important things. I have discovered over the past few years that *clarity* and *intentionality* in a leader's work genuinely matter. While I have not changed how I feel about clarity and intentionality, I felt the need to move them out of the six and embed them into every part of my life. I will get into this in a later chapter, but without extreme clarity of what matters, a leader is doomed to fail. Even with great clarity, if a leader is not intentional about what they do, the decisions they make, and the way they prioritize their time, they still may be doomed to fail. We must be mindful, as leaders, to ensure our work aligns with what we feel is important.

Allow me to share with you this disclaimer: don't think for one moment *this book* will change your school. There are a lot of suggestions in this book, but it is not the idea that changes what is happening in your school, district, or organization. YOU are the one who can and will make the difference.

I spent 26 years as a public school educator, 11 years as a classroom teacher (middle and high school), 11 years as a high school administrator (assistant and principal) and four as a superintendent. I was an athletic coach, a department chair, led lots of committees, served on state-level cabinets and boards, and so forth. I now work as a leadership coach, speaker, consultant, and publisher. I love being able to support and grow early career leaders and to bring the important message around culture and climate to schools, districts, and conferences.

Of all the amazing opportunities I had as a public educator, the one I will always cherish the most was that of being a high school principal. Heck, I still identify as a *recovering* high school principal. Not that being a principal was a bad thing or that it left me scarred for life. Rather, being a principal was the hardest, most rewarding, yet exhausting job I could ever love. There are parts of the job that I really DON'T miss such as high school dances or coordinating state testing.

However, there are parts of the job that I really miss, a lot. I miss the first day of school as a principal. Honestly, kids are never more ready to learn, and teachers are never more ready to teach than on that day! I got a ringside seat and loved it so much. I miss graduation. As the principal, I stood off stage when my kids received their diplomas. I wanted to be the first handshake, hug, and congratulations for them when they entered the world as a graduate. I have a lot of great memories from those times. What I miss most of all, though, is the time in the halls with the kids. I spent a lot of my time on a bench in the front hallway visiting with kids and staff – it was my office away from the office. My secretary, Marilyn, often said if you couldn't find me in a classroom that you'd find me on a bench. It was there that I built and cultivated lifelong relationships that I will always cherish.

In a time when education is facing unprecedented challenges, my goal with this book is to rekindle the fire around how leaders approach their work. To possibly have you step back, or step up on the balcony to see what is happening around you and for those you're charged with leading. I have written this from a set of core beliefs I hold about school leadership and what I believe matters most in the world of education. It's possible you'll agree with me, that you're already doing a lot of what I've written, and that we are kindred spirits. There is also the chance that you'll feel quite differently about leadership than I do, and that is OK. Either way, I hope this allows you to gain clarity around your core values and the intentionality in your leadership.

I am writing with the belief that we all can do something to make our schools a better place for kids and for the adults who've chosen to dedicate their lives to enriching the future of our communities. If you find one thing in this manuscript that is helpful, inspiring, or even just makes you laugh – then it was worth the time and effort.

Route 66 on the way to Oatman, AZ. Again,
not far from Kingman, AZ. What a great ride
that was in Matt Ladendecker's 2021
Corvette.

1
The Road to Awesome

*"The difficulties you meet will resolve themselves as you advance.
Proceed, and light will dawn, and shine with increasing clearness on your path."*
~ Jim Rohn

My oma (German for grandmother) was born in Germany, as was my mom, my sister, and me. In her early adult years, Oma knew the country long before the concept of East and West Germany came to be. She told the most fascinating, tear-jerking, and heart-stopping stories about her life during World War II. When she talked of having to hide from the authorities just to simply survive and make her way, along with some of her family, out of the occupied areas and to freedom, it was chilling. As she told these stories, her eyes would well up with tears and time stood still. These are not times that anyone who lived in the area could have been proud of, but they were part of what made her who she was. It certainly represents a defining event in my family's history. Listening to Oma, and others who are such great storytellers, may be why I am driven so much by the stories of others.

The same is true in education. There are so many incredible educators in the world doing so much great work. Work that impacts the lives of kids on a daily basis. These are the stories that need to be shouted from the rafters, headlining the news, and shared in our communities.

MY ROAD TO AWESOME STORY

I grew up in a normal, middle-class family in central Wyoming. I am the middle child, having both an older and younger sister. I was the kid who flew under the radar. You know, not super popular but also not an outcast. I had several really good friends as I made my way through school and felt I was a normal kid. I was involved at my school, played two different sports, attended games and dances, and even had a girlfriend or two along the way.

I don't believe I had any clear path in my mind regarding what I wanted to do with my life. If you had asked me what I wanted to be when I grew up, I would probably not have had a quality answer. I might have considered being a professional tennis player, but I wasn't that great of a player. Definitely, not the best on my team. It turned out I wasn't even the best player in my family – that title belongs to my younger sister.

The high school I attended was pretty big, and it was decided the students would have a random staff member as an advisor. My advisor was a wonderful woman and the mother of one of my friends. She was also the school nurse, so she wasn't exactly a fountain of information when it came to prepping for life after high school. I am confident we had guidance counselors, real, actual counselors at the school, but I couldn't have picked them out of line-up at the time. As my senior year of high school was winding down, I was faced with the reality of what to do next. I knew that I would go to college; it was never said out loud, but I knew it was an expectation my parents had for all three of us kids. I ultimately decided to major in physical therapy based on a moment from my sophomore year.

NOVEMBER 23, 1984

I would be shocked if you remember this date specifically. I had to look it up myself (thanks, Google). One of my most vivid memories from high school occurred on this date. I was not only a tennis player but also a basketball player, in the loosest sense of the word. I was on the team, but that's about the extent of my basketball career for any highlights. In fact, I spent more time on the training room floor, table, and slant boards than I ever did in an actual game. I had some pretty tough luck as a high school athlete when it came to injuries. I severely sprained my right ankle multiple times (ending up on crutches a couple of those times), badly sprained my right wrist, and had multiple issues with my quadriceps muscles. This all added up to quite a bit of time with John Noffsinger, or Trainer John as he was known to all of the athletes at Kelly Walsh High. November 23, 1984 was no different. As a sophomore in high school, my season was actually off to a great start. I was slated to be in the starting lineup and was playing better than I ever had before. I was confident and really fit well into Coach Meeboer's offense. This is where the first ankle injury comes into play. Our final practice before the season opener was a walk-through and should not have been a time for injury. Unfortunately, as I came off a screen, I caught the ball and squared up, took the shot (all net) and landed awkwardly on somebody's foot, turning my ankle. This earned me my first trip to the training room. I would become a regular guest in that room.

The normal rehab for my ankle injury included before and after practice in the ice bath, on the slant board, and of course taping. On November 23rd, after practice, I was in the training room cutting off my tape and preparing to immerse my foot in the ice bath. There were probably 10 of us in the room, with the Boston College vs. Miami football game on in the background. It was just another day after practice when it happened. Doug Flutie had pulled off one of the greatest plays in the history of college football. And I saw it live on TV in the training room.

As the realization of picking a career pathway began to settle in, I tried to reflect on my life at the time, all 17 years of it. I had no idea what I wanted to do except that I would be attending the local community college. As I spent time thinking about what interested me, reflecting on that memory drove me to have an interest in athletic training. What a great life Trainer John had going for himself. He got to be a part of high school athletics, built relationships with students and coaches, and had a TV in his office. My path was identified. I wanted to be a high school athletic trainer.

I never really got in trouble in high school nor did I skip a class. In fact, I even went to two of my classes on senior ditch day (it was the only way mom would excuse me from the other classes). Unfortunately for me, I wasn't as ready for college as I should have been after graduation. I discovered that nobody is checking on you, and you're free to choose whether or not to actually show up to class. I was a disaster. I was having fun, A LOT OF FUN!! I was arguably the best pool player on campus. I certainly wasn't putting in any effort to pass a class. As a result, I struggled in college, which is a mild way of saying I flunked out of my first semester of college.

I decided to change my major, twice, to no avail. I even dropped out, got married and decided I would be a working man. It didn't take long to realize that retail sales was not going to be a lifelong, fulfilling dream, so I decided to go back to college. Mind you, I still had no direction, but my wife at that time convinced me to get myself together. Without her pushing me to find something I was passionate about and helping me understand the difference between just having a job and having a career, I am not sure where I would have ended up. Shortly after going back to school, the moment I needed came my way, and it was pivotal.

A friend asked me if, since I had played basketball, I would help him coach a team. A fifth grade girls basketball team. I eagerly agreed and found the passion and focus I desperately needed. Within days I had changed my major again, this time to secondary education. The high quantity of science courses I had taken, and the few I'd passed, while majoring in physical therapy were paying off with my concentration areas being Biology and Chemistry. While not everything was perfectly smooth from that point on, including a divorce from my previously mentioned wife, I was able to graduate and land my first teaching job in Kingman, Arizona.

I spent 11 years as a classroom teacher, the first five as a junior high science teacher and the following six as a high school science teacher. As you can imagine, I had a number of students in my class for more than one course over their school careers. Sarah was one of those students. She was in my class as an eighth

15

grader and then again in 10th - 12th grade each year. It was clear early on that Sarah had a passion for science and wanted to take every science class she could possibly take. Even in junior high, her interests leaned toward the medical field. We had many conversations about her interests during her time as a student. While I could tell her story, it might be better to see it from her perspective.

— — — — — — — —

POINT OF VIEW – SARAH BRADY

Pep was the teacher who wanted to get to know something special about each of his students, learn what motivated them and create a student-teacher relationship that promoted academic excellence. I latched onto his enthusiastic teaching and his high expectations and high accountability attitude. He was the teacher everyone wanted to please, he was quick to praise in public and would discuss any shortcomings in private. This student-teacher relationship resulted in higher grades and engaged students.

I always had a desire to have a career in the medical field. My sophomore year I took the AP Biology courses that were offered as well as Medical Terminology and decided to go through a school program to obtain my Certified Nursing Assistant (CNA) license. I started working as a CNA 20 hrs per week at a local nursing home and fell in love with patient care. I was disappointed that my high school didn't offer any human science courses such as Anatomy and Physiology. I expressed this to Pep, and somehow, he made it happen the next year! My junior and senior year he personally taught Anatomy & Physiology. I loved these courses and had a blast learning these subjects. Looking back on that, this small course addition helped confirm my love of the human body and how it worked and solidified my course in life to become a Registered Nurse.

I became a Registered Nurse at age 21 and remember joking with some of my elderly patients, who didn't think I looked old enough to be their nurse, that I was able to provide narcotic pain medication before I could legally walk into a bar and order a drink. This was a fun way to break the ice with my patients. I have since completed my Bachelor's of Science in Nursing and my Master's in Organizational Leadership. I am currently the Director of Intensive Care at my local hospital.

In 2010 I was able to participate in a non-profit medical mission organization called Live Now Inc. and travel to Tanzania to provide free health care, assist with surgical procedures, post-op care and teaching.

— — — — — — — —

We should be working to help others find and pursue their passions. Share your passions and pay close attention to the passions of your students. Encourage them, and help them find their way to the passions they wish to pursue.

An interesting thing happens when you become a teacher. You spend a great deal of time in college preparing for your first classroom. Then, when you get that first classroom, you realize you have NO idea what you are doing. We want to believe we are fully prepared to start teaching from day one, but really, you don't learn how to teach until YOU do the teaching.

I arrived in Kingman excited to begin my career and under the leadership of one of the best mentors, leaders, and education heroes I have met in my life – my first principal, Betsy Parker. As a first year teacher, I wanted my principal to help me grow, be a better teacher, and to be patient with me as I found my way. What I actually got from my first principal was far beyond that – I was given a life-long friendship, someone to look up to, someone who would say something that would impact me the rest of my life. I didn't consider myself a leader. I was a guy who went with the flow, you SHOULDN'T have been following me. But Betsy saw something different. She saw me for what I could be, not just what I was. Betsy saw me as a leader. I'm pretty sure she was the first person I ever heard say that I had leadership skills, and I was inspired!

TWO QUESTIONS

Two questions were asked. Two questions that are simple in nature, yet have incredible depth. Two questions that on the surface should be common sense but, in reality, represent a massive paradigm shift. Two questions asked in a 10-second window that changed me forever.

After 11 years in the classroom and living over 13 hours away from my hometown, my family and I decided we would move away from Arizona and back to Wyoming. I was fortunate enough to land an assistant principal position at a really great school in the southwest part of the state. My role would be to oversee all discipline and attendance. I was fired up!

I learned rather quickly the expectations the staff had for me in my new job. I was to kick butt and take no prisoners. The staff wanted strict discipline and for kids to comply with their orders. I found, too, that our leadership team wanted our teachers to behave similarly. Do what you are told, don't complain. I fell right into this culture and, before long, found I was using the same language used by my peers. The message was clear, let's catch them (meaning everyone) doing things wrong. Punishment will gain compliance, right? This is the single WORST leadership strategy known to man. Punishment to gain compliance doesn't work.

A little over halfway through that school year we held a staff meeting to discuss solutions to the two biggest problems in education, as we saw it. You know these crucial conversations happen often. The two big questions:
1. *What are we going to do about hats?*
2. *What are we going to do about cell phones?*

No, these are not *the* two questions I've been referring to so far, but these sure are critical in the race for awesome, high-engagement lessons right? NO, not at all, but here we were, spending valuable time on two things I found ridiculous (and still do). Come on teachers, come on administrators - treat your kids with respect, develop engaging lessons so kids will pay attention to their learning, not their technology. When you treat kids like grown ups, they will often act like grown ups.

Yes, we want our students to be respectful adults and want them engaged with their learning, but we were going about this the wrong way. Here we sat, in another meeting discussing what consequences we could take, or threaten to take, that would make kids put away the technology, take off the hat, and be angelic students from 8 am to 3 pm. UGH!!

Then it happened. *I was asked two questions.* They hit me like lightning. One of the school social workers, we will call her Spring, because that's her name, raised her hand and politely asked,

"Why does it always have to be about what they do wrong?"

Spring followed up that one with another glass-shattering query,

"Why can't it be about what they do right?"

The reaction in the room was mixed, some nodding their heads seeming to say, "Yeah, what she said," while others looked as if someone just notified them the IRS was auditing their last 10 years worth of tax returns. Me, I was speechless.

I'm not sure how it happened, but somehow, I'd become someone I really didn't like. I look back at it now, and I was an absolute JERK. I was proud of the way I could catch kids doing the wrong things, that I knew where to hide to catch them in the act – it was like a game. It had nothing to do with learning (the whole purpose of school, by the way). It was about me being superior to the kids at my school. Wow, I really hate that guy!

Spring's words changed how I looked at my job. In an instant, I found myself wondering why in the world I thought my behavior had been OK. I wish I could apologize to a lot of the kids I punished that year. I knew one thing though, I had a chance to fix it going forward. It was time to change not only the culture and climate of our school but the way we were leading. And I had company. Several of the staff felt the same way – it was time for game-changing school leadership, and we would never be the same!!

Me in my Jeep in the foothills of White
Mountain in Rock Springs, WY. My wife and
I didn't have time to go all the way up the
mountain, but wanted a quick Jeep ride. This
turned out being a really fun ride through all
of the ravines.

2
Reimagining School Leadership

"If your actions inspire others to dream more, learn more, do more and become more, you are a leader."
~ John Quincy Adams

During my first year as the principal at Rock Springs High School (RSHS), I was asked to visit some model schools in another state with my superintendent and a couple of other principals from our district. On the return trip, I sat on the plane with two people I'd never met before. You've all been in this situation and you know there are two options for the flight. You can put in your AirPods, lean against the wall of the plane, and pretend to be asleep or you can engage in polite conversation with your new friends for the next couple hours. In this case, I decided to visit a little bit. The lady sitting next to me was an inexperienced flier and was chatty from the time she sat down. She told me about how she was flying for business, was currently an advertising agent for a small software company, and that she had two kids. The third member of our row party was dialed in to some work on his laptop computer and seemed disinterested in the two of us.

At one point, my now long-time acquaintance took a breath and let me talk a little about who I was. I told her about where I lived (she had no clue people actually lived in Wyoming) and what I did for a living. I'm sure this wasn't her exact reaction, but I've seen, heard, and felt this reaction so many times that it has probably amalgamated itself into one universal move. When I told her I was a high school principal, she looked at me with her head tilted to the side and a sad, sympathetic expression on her face and said "Oh, I'm sorry."

OK, wait. You're sorry? **Why is being the principal worthy of your sympathy?** I got this all the time. When meeting parents for the first time they would tell me their student's name and say, "You probably don't know her, she's a good kid." AHHHH! This just drove me crazy. I KNEW THE GOOD KIDS!! Actually, they were all good, some just needed a lot more love.

This reaction to meeting the principal, whether your kid is at my school or not, comes from a place of long-outdated experience.

The truth is, being a school leader is all about knowing your kids and your adults. Too often, parents base their beliefs of what a principal does on their own school experience. The role of the principal has changed more dramatically than any position in schools. The principal is not, exclusively, the disciplinarian. In today's schools the principal is expected to be an instructional leader, a relationship builder, a cheerleader, a manager, an expert in human resources, a financial planner, a communicator, a therapist (for adults and kids alike), a coach, an evaluator, a custodian, and, in some unfortunate cases, a surrogate parent.

Like many new principals, I was not taking my first principal role in a new building. I'd already been working in the building as an assistant principal, so the move from my office to the principal's office was a mere 40 feet. But it might as well have been 40 miles. When you switch from one role to the other, it is astounding how big the change is. My predecessor referred to the roles of his three assistant principals as sandboxes. He told us often to try and stay in our own sandbox but, if we stray, to make sure we clean up any mess we make in someone else's sandbox. He also stressed that our sandboxes were all in his sandbox.

My first official day on the job was July 5, 2011, but I was in the office before that wondering aloud, "What now?" Sure, I had been an assistant principal for five years, at this point I was ready, right? NO, no I wasn't, and if anyone reading this says they were ready for their first principalship, I'm calling you out. In my interview only a few days earlier I had asked the committee what they wanted from me if I were chosen to lead the school. I believe there were 10 or 12 people on the committee, and I can't tell you what any of them said except for the superintendent. His words were, "I need you to be the instructional leader of that school." OK, cool – but I already was the instructional leader, that was my role as the assistant principal. What does that mean? Do I just keep doing what I was doing? Was I doing it wrong? What else am I supposed to do? Where are these sandboxes again?

I spent the better part of July fourth in my new office mapping out what the job descriptions (sandboxes) of the three assistant principals on my team would be and how I would lead their work. Here is where I began to fail. I had the belief that I had to have all the answers. After all, I was hired to do this job, to lead. I better get to it and start leading. The reality was, I had already been leading but from a different role.

Leadership is never about a title, and just because your title changes doesn't mean your style of leadership should change.

I was only the third principal at the school in 35 years. My predecessor had been principal for 17 years, his predecessor 18 years. Like most first-time principals, I had a desire to make the job my own, to put my stamp on the building so to speak. In trying so hard not to be the guy before me, I overlooked some really great work he had put in place and a leadership system that truly was effective. It took some time for me to start seeing the errors I was making, but once things began unraveling, they were obvious. I was trying to do it all, to be the smartest person in the room, to have all the answers. *You don't have to do it alone.*

When I was a sophomore in high school, I was a starter on the basketball team and probably thought I was the center of the universe. During our basketball unit in PE we were playing a 5 on 5 tournament in class. I was the point guard, the shooter, the rebounder, I did it all. Apparently, I felt the need to demonstrate just how good I was as a player. My PE teacher taught me a great lesson that day. He slowly took one player from my team off the floor without me knowing. I was a total ball-hog!! At one point during the game, the other team had scored, and I stood around waiting for someone to pass the ball in – my entire team was sitting on the sidelines watching me. I couldn't even tell you who was on my team because I had made it all about me. My first year as a principal was a lot like this. I felt I had to do it all and would get frustrated with my assistants because they weren't doing anything. That was on me. I had gotten so lost in all the work that I had forgotten, or failed to learn, just what my role really was. I forgot to lead.

My second year as a principal began with a new superintendent. The previous superintendent had retired and our school board decided the district could move forward best by having someone come from the outside with fresh ideas. Unfortunately, that person's tenure as superintendent was fairly short-lived, ending rather controversially after 15 bumpy months. But, it was not all bad, at least from my perspective.

The superintendent came in with many ideas he'd learned from other districts in his time, and his best idea by far was to provide coaching for all the school and district administrators. Coaching has not always received the best reception in the world of education. Many teachers and administrators believe coaching is only for those who are the biggest of messes. The reception in my district was not much different, with nearly all administrators feeling slighted or doubted by having a coach assigned to them. I was one of the few who were excited by the idea. I knew I needed some help and welcomed having someone with experience to assist me in my role.

Sometimes, the best thing a leader can do is acknowledge what they don't know.

My leadership coach, Tom, like Betsy, is one of the most important people and mentors I have encountered in my career.

Tom was a middle school principal in Colorado at the time we met. I believed I could be not only good at what I did but that I could be great. To this point, I wasn't living up to my expectations and felt I was forever breathing through a snorkel with my head well below the level of the water. Tom was the model of what a principal should be in terms of how he worked with people, trusted his team, and interacted with his community. I met Tom at his school in Colorado. We spent a little over an hour getting acquainted, and I just knew he would be someone that could help me get things back in order. Tom was going to help me be the leader I knew I could be.

Tom came and visited me in the fall of that year, and the day was a mess. We met in the parking lot and walked in together. Between the front doors and my office, which was a fairly short walk, I was stopped by five teachers asking for something, had multiple requests for things from students, and my pushpin board (hanging outside my office) had probably nine notes pinned to it. A group of parents were waiting to see me, angry about something in one of our science classrooms, and insisted they weren't leaving until I gave them my time. The bell had yet to ring, and my day (a Monday, by the way) was off to a flying start. This might seem like a wild scenario, but this was just another day in the life of my principalship. By 10:30 I had met all the requests of the teachers who needed me, answered most of the notes on the board, and had convinced the parents to meet with one of my assistant principals. Tom and I finally had a minute to talk. I expected we would sit down, drink a cup of coffee, and talk shop (I had no idea what to expect from a coach). Tom handed me a notebook, a pen, and we left my office. We walked down one of the many hallways at my high school where, at random, he chose a classroom, and we went in.

After about 10 minutes in the classroom, Tom stepped into the hallway motioning for me to follow. His question to me was,

"What did you see?" I was a bit taken off guard by this. Sure, I did walk-through observations and gave feedback, but he wanted to compare notes, which we did. We went to another classroom, then another, and another. Then, we went to lunch. I was so confused!!! There were a million things I needed to be doing in my office; what were we doing in classrooms? I needed him to help me be a better principal, not teach me how to do walk-throughs. I knew how to do that!

I finally worked up the courage at lunch to ask Tom when we were going to get to the important work of being a principal. Why was it he thought we needed to observe my teachers when clearly I had a lot of other things to learn? Tom took a breath, smiled a little, and said maybe the most profound thing I had heard since becoming the principal, **"Darrin, you need to stop being a firefighter, and start being a leader, and I'm here to help you do that."**

As a school leader, I had it in my head that my job was to solve everybody's problems. I needed to be the sole owner of information, the smartest person in the room. I had not given any responsibilities to my assistant principals. I wasn't using my office manager anywhere near to her capacity, leaving her feeling useless, and I was killing myself trying to do it all. Tom taught me, among many things, that a leader is not someone who does it all but is someone who empowers others to do awesome things by trusting them, coaching them, and guiding them.

WHAT IT ALL MEANS

So, what does it mean to be a school leader? The traditional role definition tells us a school leader is someone who manages the school, is responsible for disciplining students, hiring teachers, and various other tasks. The principal in the post-NCLB era is portrayed as the person who knows data, helps improve instruction, and spends all their time in classrooms *where the action is.*

I was able to work with Tom as my leadership coach for two years. In that time, I really felt like I had learned a substantial amount about shifting from what is on fire to what is really important in the daily grind of being the principal. Tom taught me much about leading from the balcony. It is important for leaders to take that walk up onto the balcony and see the whole picture of their school, district, or organization. The best leaders will build systems that are effectively independent of the person leading the system. Those leaders understand that the operational side of their school or district is just as important as the instructional side. Where I had failed early on was believing that being the instructional leader was THE work, and being the instructional leader included solving everyone's problems and challenges. During my two years with Tom, I learned how to really be a school leader. I learned what really mattered to me as a leader, not just to Tom. Interestingly, I learned that I wasn't the only school leader who had these struggles. In fact, nearly every principal will tell you (if they are honest about it) how difficult being the principal is and how very little preparation for the job comes from a masters degree program or classroom instructional experience. The fact is, being a principal is a very hard job, and we all struggle with various parts of the role. Most principals are, truly, not that well prepared when they land that first job. I was so intrigued by my experience as a struggling principal and the growth I had working with Tom that I wrote a dissertation on the topic.

There is much we get right about school leadership. Our profession has changed drastically in the past two decades, in both positive and less than desirable ways. Increased opportunities in professional development for teachers have given us so many more tools to impact student learning.

Accountability measures and pandemic era learning loss have so many educators and pundits concentrating on test scores as the only metric (or seemingly so) by which our level of success or failure is calculated. Increased focus on earning academic and athletic scholarships have laser-focused some parents away from the joy of learning and competing to blame. Students are driven to be *successful* by the definitions created by people other than themselves and struggle with their own sense of belonging and mental well-being. Pressure to perform is everywhere - on students, teachers, parents, and squarely on the shoulders of the principal. It is my hope that this book will help principals, as well as teachers, parents, students, and others to take a look at their perspective. Go stand on the balcony and think about what is happening in your school community. Is it what you really wanted when you chose this profession? It's time that school leaders take a step back and think about what really matters.

— — — — — — — —

POINT OF VIEW – ERIC LILLIS

If you think the job of high school principal is easy, then you are just fooling yourself. It is also one of the most fulfilling and rewarding positions in ALL of education. You have a front row seat to some of the most amazing events and instances that you will ever encounter as an educator. A high school principal is not a passenger on the bus, a high school principal is DRIVING the bus.

Now, here is the challenge - how do you get students, staff, and parents on board that bus with you?

I was basically an interim high school principal for two years. I came into the position almost by accident. I had been working in the Office of Curriculum and Instruction, when our executive director called me into her office, shut the door, and said, "I need you to be the principal at the High School, and I need an answer today." Wow!! After I picked myself up off of the floor, I immediately left campus to speak to my wife, then went to speak to my Pastor. Both of whom encouraged me to go for it. I accepted the position, went home that night and immediately began making a list of all of the changes that I wanted to make at the high school. Whoa, Eric, easy. You are entering a school that already has a strong climate and culture, solid teachers, and amazing kids. How hard can this be and how many changes do you really think you need to make? Time to put a little thought into this before you turn this place upside down, confuse students and anger staffulty with a massive amount of change.

So, I stepped back, spent some time in the high school talking to students, staffulty and parents about what THEY would like to see at our high school, then began formulating some ideas for positive change. Leadership is not just about your name on the door (even though I really did have my name on the door), leadership is about listening to those around you and including your stakeholders in the decision making process. Additionally, I did not want to be the school principal who sat behind the desk, sending 10 emails a day and never having a conversation with, nor ever listening to, students and staffulty. I wanted to be visible. I wanted to be in the hallways and in the classrooms forming relationships day after day. Leadership is also about letting others know that you are there. That you are present. That those around you feel like they are seen. And what they do each day, what they are all about, has value. There are SO MANY responsibilities and managerial tasks that a school leader encounters every day. I decided to just prioritize. Hear and listen to your staffulty and students, be seen regularly, and develop those positive relationships that are important for any leader to develop. Once those things are done, your stakeholders will get on the bus and ride it with you in any direction and to any destination.

After this two-year interim position as a high school principal, I now have the task of leading a school district as Executive Director. I have the opportunity to lead a very academically-strong set of schools, all of which have outstanding leadership, fantastic students and supportive parents. But it is also a school district that is stuck in a traditional way of doing things. My philosophy and my priorities will not *change and simply cannot change. I will continue to lead by listening, lead by being seen across campus, and lead by forming relationships across the school district. Establishing relationships and mutual respect and trust with those around you will ease the process of change.*

— — — — — — — —

A MODEL FOR SCHOOL LEADERSHIP

I find it interesting how many books have been launched about improving schools and student performance. Books about leadership, instruction, using data, and research-based practices fill the shelves of my office. Some of these are fantastic books and have shifted the landscape of quality student learning. My passion is for meaningful and impactful leadership, not only for student learning but for the betterment of people. We are in the people business, don't ever forget that. So, if our efforts are simply to improve test scores or the percentages of kids who graduate from high school there is a fairly decent chance we are missing the point.

We never should evaluate a kid, or a teacher for that matter, simply on a set of test scores. This could easily be a 10 page diatribe on why I think test scores are among the most flawed data sets in history. However, I'll keep the focus on how leadership can be impactful on people. It is from this place where I lead on a daily basis. My leadership beliefs are rooted in a passion for bringing positivity and decency back to our society. What drives me to do the work I do, what motivated me to write and update this book, what makes me speak with, coach, and grow leaders of all kinds are these six core beliefs.

The Best Leaders

KNOW IT IS CRITICAL TO BUILD AND MAINTAIN A POSITIVE CULTURE AND CLIMATE IN THEIR SCHOOL.

KNOW THEY MUST VALUE, SUPPORT, AND CARE FOR EVERYONE ON THEIR STAFF.

EMPOWER AND EMBRACE STUDENT VOICE.

PRIORITIZE BEING THE INSTRUCTIONAL LEADER OF THEIR ORGANIZATION.

KNOW THAT LEADING WITH A COACHING MINDSET WILL BRING OUT THE BEST IN ALL THEIR STAFF.

ARE THE CHAMPIONS OF THEIR ORGANIZATIONS.

This may appear as a leadership manifesto, and in many ways, that's exactly what it is. Traditional models of school leadership where one person or just a couple people own the knowledge, direction, and goals of the organization are outdated and inefficient. If you really want Road to Awesome leadership to happen in your school, you have to be willing to open your circle and give away some of the control. Think about everyone who is impacted by the daily work of your schools. I challenge you to empower your teachers, students, and community members to lead the school with you.

In the coming chapters I will push you to be clear and intentional with your values, your vision for your school, and how you will work to ensure continuous improvement. I will challenge you to build an awesome culture and climate, ignite the awesome in your staff and students, and be the champion of your school.

It's time to reimagine school leadership, then DO SOMETHING ABOUT IT!

My wife, daughter and our dog decided to
drive the back way to Lander, WY from Rock
Springs, WY for a weekend getaway. The trees
were blazing with their fall reds and yellows.

3

Being Clear,
Being Intentional

*"Leadership is the capacity to translate
vision into reality."*
~ Warren G. Bennis

As a basketball coach, I was blessed to coach some wonderful kids and amazing athletes. There was one school that, no matter what we did or which sport I was coaching (I also coached tennis and football), I could not beat – Ironwood High School. In my second year as the girls varsity basketball coach, we played Ironwood on our home floor, and with less than 20 seconds left in the game, we had the ball in a tie game. I called a time-out and instructed my team (on the little white board of course) to run a pick-and-roll play off the inbounds. I told Rachel and Lindsay exactly how I wanted it to run. It was a play they'd run well all season. As we left the huddle, Lindsay asked me if she was setting or receiving the screen. Not listening well, I said, "You're receiving it," and on to the floor she went. The play set up perfectly as we came out of the huddle and got the ball in. Unfortunately, I had switched the roles of the two players in the huddle, which is why Lindsay had asked the question. The way they'd run it all year had Lindsay setting the screen, then rolling to the basket. I didn't listen to my players, and we ended up turning the ball over. Ironwood scored at the buzzer to send us to the locker room with a very frustrating loss. A loss that, in my mind, was 100% on my shoulders.

I learned something about myself that night. Not just that I was cursed by the crimson scourge (their main school color was red) known as the Ironwood Eagles (I did finally beat them), I learned that I needed to be crystal clear about what I expected, what my intentions were and to ensure that I had been heard correctly. I also discovered that I have to listen to hear, not simply to respond. Had I been listening for understanding, I would have realized that I had switched the roles and would have reversed the set up. Maybe we would have won, maybe not. The point is, as leaders, we have to listen to hear and to understand.

THE IMPORTANCE OF CLARITY

In my first year as the building principal, I laid out what I expected of my leadership team on their first day back – or so I thought. I found myself faced with push-back against the number of classroom walkthroughs, the process I had laid out for evaluation, job expectations, and much more. I was quite frustrated but came to understand it was my lack of a plan for how it was all to be accomplished. I am not a systems thinker. I am much more of what Robert Jordan would call a strategist leader. In Wagner and Jordan's book *Right Leader, Right Time: Discover Your Leadership Style for a Winning Career and Company*, they discuss four leadership styles. The strategist leader will be someone who creates ideas to scale and will rely upon the members of the team to make these ideas a reality. I neither shared nor gave the team the opportunity to create these expectations. I didn't allow them to work collaboratively with me to develop the plan. That led to a lack of clarity. Honestly, I probably wasn't clear either on what it was I really wanted from them.

As I continued on my leadership journey, one thing became more and more evident. I had to be clear about what I expected and provide clarity in the directions or actions I wished to see happening. This was true in the classrooms, in our behavior management, and in building our culture. As a leader, it is critical to take the time necessary to make your intentions, expectations, and desires crystal clear.

WELL, WHAT DID YOU EXPECT?

I was working with a first year teacher, discussing her first formal observation. There were a lot of positives, yet the level of engagement and student behavior wasn't what I would like to see in a classroom. During the conversation I asked her if the behaviors I had observed met with her expectations of her students. Pure silence. She really didn't know what to say because she hadn't thought about what she expected of her students. I am not saying she was wrong, rather she was unprepared to be in this position without some help and some coaching.

Clarity of what we expect is essential and should match with our values and what we hold important. We have to be clear in what we expect before we can ever hold someone to those expectations. I struggled a little in the above situation because I felt I had failed the young teacher by not helping her have clear student expectations before the year began. Fortunately, it was early enough for her to recover and grow in that area, which she did.

CLARITY OF VALUES
Similar to the basketball story above, it is imperative that leaders are clear on their beliefs and values. It's said you've got to stand for something or you'll fall for everything. These are the things you'll stand on the table for, bang your fist on the wall, and refuse to back away. I've already shared my core values that drive my leadership.

Each of the next six chapters provide greater clarity and some stories behind why I hold them close. I feel my values revolve around the idea that we're in the people business. Focusing on the human being first – their potential, their personal needs, and their value – is the lens I choose to look through as a leader. I have been on the other side of it, having worked with and for others who didn't necessarily lead from this place.

KNOW IT IS CRITICAL TO BUILD AND MAINTAIN A POSITIVE CULTURE AND CLIMATE IN THEIR SCHOOL.

KNOW THEY MUST VALUE, SUPPORT, AND CARE FOR EVERYONE ON THEIR STAFF.

EMPOWER AND EMBRACE STUDENT VOICE.

The Best Leaders

PRIORITIZE BEING THE INSTRUCTIONAL LEADER OF THEIR ORGANIZATION.

KNOW THAT LEADING WITH A COACHING MINDSET WILL BRING OUT THE BEST IN ALL THEIR STAFF.

ARE THE CHAMPIONS OF THEIR ORGANIZATIONS.

Another key element in this development of clarity is how we communicate our values and expectations. I learned quickly that telling someone, or an entire staff meeting full of people, what you expect one time does not cut it. Just because I said it once does not mean they heard it. Telling students something once rarely leads to the whole class understanding and meeting the guidelines of an assignment. Leading adults is no different. Be clear about what you value, what you expect, and continually share those with the people you lead.

BEING INTENTIONAL

Identifying your values and your expectations is a crucial step to becoming one of the best leaders. However, if the use of time and selection of our actions on a daily basis doesn't align with those values and expectations, odds are we won't live up to them and neither will those around us. When I work with school and district leaders, I ask what it is that they value and what they expect from their students and staff. Then, I go and ask the same questions of their staff and students about the leader. If they don't know, the leader hasn't done enough to wear those values and expectations on their sleeve.

If being in the classrooms as the instructional leader is important, you'll let everyone know that is what you are doing. You'll tell them not to interrupt you while you are doing classroom observations, meeting with teachers, or giving feedback. I learned from Tom to put those values and expectations to the forefront of my work. I posted goals in my office, shared expectations and what I felt was important with staff, students, and community whenever the opportunity came my way. I scheduled regular check in time with myself. I would actually stand on the balcony in the gym and think through where I was with the things that were important to me, and evaluate how I was allocating my time for these important areas of work.

As a leader, you have only so much time in a day. I would block time on my calendar every week to ensure I was putting in the work on culture, instructional leadership, and into the relationships that were so pivotal to our success as a school. The best leaders are going to be very intentional with their use of time. It is too precious of a commodity to leave to chance. Put your priorities on the calendar, protect them, and it becomes clear to those around you what you value, what you expect, and how you will lead. This will be evident because your actions will match your words.

LISTENING IS LOVING

As valuable as it is to visit classrooms when the students are present, consider visiting when kids aren't there as well. There are definitely times when meeting with a teacher in the leader's office is more appropriate. But that should be the only time the leader's office is the chosen destination for meetings. When possible, leaders should go to the staff member's location rather than their own office. Summoning someone to your office can imply that your time is more valuable than theirs. Leaders have more flexibility in their schedules than teachers. If a meeting is needed, schedule it for the teacher's prep time, and go to their space. It will create a lot less anxiety and increase the time you are out and visible to others.

I was an open book to my staff, they probably all had my cell phone number and knew they could text or call me any time. I occasionally received a text or an email requesting a meeting with me. I always asked when and told them I would go to them for our meeting. I once got an email from an elementary teacher asking to meet with me. I followed the usual protocol and set up time to go see her during the following week. I had been told by her principal she wanted to take an extra day off after a holiday. In my district, like many others, only the superintendent can approve this time off. I could have emailed her, but instead, I kept the meeting. She shared her request, which I approved happily. It was the next thing I did that was impactful and left a lasting impression on me. I asked her, knowing she was having a tough year with some high behavioral and social-emotionally challenged students, a very basic question: **How are you doing?**

Her response began with her biting her lip and tears welling in her eyes. The content of our conversation will remain between the two of us, but it's important to never forget that sometimes people just want to have someone listen to them and demonstrate how much they care. My wife and daughter would confirm that I'm an easy cry. Soon, both the teacher and I were in tears. Not looking for solutions, just sharing struggles and successes of our most at-risk students. At the end of the conversation I asked her what I could do to help. Her answer was, "**This. Just come listen to me.**"

LIVING THE VISION OUT LOUD
I grew up on a double dead–end street. Yes, my street went absolutely nowhere, which made it a great place to be a kid. We played whatever sport was happening at a given time of year in the street. We didn't have officials, usually didn't have the correct number of players, and certainly didn't have fancy uniforms. We just played, and played, and played until finally our moms called us in for dinner. Today, specialization seems to be the norm and kids participate in club sports and other activities that take parents all over the country for weekend competition.

My daughter's experience in school was no different. With Liz as a competitive dance team member, we put thousands of miles on our cars over the better part of eight years. I didn't mind the dance competitions, they afforded me a lot of time to work on course work and papers for my doctorate degree. Another bonus to many of these weekend ventures was their locations. This provided me an opportunity to venture around the school buildings and see what stories were being told.

YOUR WALLS ARE TALKING – WHAT ARE THEY SAYING?

Walk in the front door of any school, even your own. What do you see? If the building is familiar to you it's possible you don't even notice what is on the walls – the paint, the posters, even the trophies in the cases. But what do people who visit your school see? The walls are talking to them; think about the stories being told, or being missed.

My interest in the look of schools probably dates back to being a first year teacher. When I first arrived in Kingman, the school year was still a few weeks off, but I couldn't wait to be in my very own classroom. I went to the school and got a quick tour which ended in Room 205. There wasn't much in that room. Over the next 10 days I proceeded to cover nearly every inch of wall space with posters (movies, athletes, sports teams) showing my students who I was and what I was interested in. Michael Jordan and John Elway dominated the space.

Betsy had one rule when it came to wrapping up the year and checking out for the summer. Your classroom walls better be completely bare, all posters had to come down. This gave our custodial team easy access to the walls for summer cleaning. Some of my fellow teachers didn't like that rule and pushed back every spring. I wasn't in that camp. I loved getting to set the room up each August and always had some new wall swag to share my interests.

When I became a school administrator, I really didn't have the chance to decorate my room. Sure, I had an office, but that was a *professional space*. I still decorated the office, but not anything like my classroom. The reality is when you are the school leader, the atmosphere and the look of the school is on you. You can be the one to set the tone of your school's appearance and the vision it reflects.

The summer of my first year as the building principal, I was able to really begin shifting the look of our school. A student, Aly, asked me if she could paint a quote on the wall.

At the end of our main hallway was a large display case we had started using to splash pictures of our students on a television screen in a revolving slideshow. Above the case was some blank (and rather ugly) brown 70's paneling. This was where Aly had decided her quote should be painted. We covered the paneling in black paint (one of the school colors), and Aly painted her quote in orange (the other school color).

One day your life will flash before your eyes,
make sure it's worth watching.
~ Gerard Way

Quotes like these became quite popular, and students came to me frequently with ideas for other quotes and their locations. The quotes quickly evolved into murals. A mural project has been in place for many years in which the senior art students paint a large mural on one of the walls of the school to be signed by all graduates at the end of the year. It is an awesome tradition. Along with this, I wanted our walls to reflect who the kids and adults were DURING the time they were there, not just at the end.

Our walls were boring, they were telling absolutely NO stories. Nothing about the walls could tell a visitor what was important to us, what we stood for, or what we saw as the vision of our school.

A group of us came together and met at the front door of our school that summer. We decided to walk in together and discuss what our hallways were telling us. What we found were boring, tan brick walls. The benches at least said that we value our kids as human beings, but not much more than that. There were no quotes in the front hallway, except for Aly's.

We decided that in order to reach all kids, we wanted something that spoke to us – seeing our kids as who they were. Not just as students but who they were as people. We wanted to reflect their interests, their values, and for the hallway to be about who the current students were, not just those who came before.

I worked with our maintenance supervisor to have all the bricks in the front hall painted in a variety of colors, giving us a great amount of canvas on which to create. Upwards of 20 - 30 students showed up at various times to put in the effort needed to transform the space. The end product was truly remarkable and left everyone commenting on *the walls that speak*.

Over a period of several years, murals and quotes similar to these continued to show up all over the school. Once our students and teachers had permission to make the school their space, we began seeing more and more of this type of effort. There are some things to keep in mind if you choose to follow this path. Don't copy something you see from another school or on social media. Make certain this work reflects you and your school's values, what you believe in, and the vision of the school. Make it tell a story about your kids, your community, or something significant. Just like with any other initiative or undertaking, without a clear vision or plan, it's just paint.

A two-track road on top of White Mountain
in Rock Springs, WY. This trip included my
wife and her parents. We were lucky enough
to see quite a few herds of wild horses that
make their home on White Mountain.

4
The Pulse of Your School

*"One's vision is not a roadmap
but a compass."*
~ Peter Block

When I was in college, I worked as a retail salesman for a well-known department store. My job was to sell hardware, tools, mowers, tractors, and the like. I was fairly good at the job, but in all honesty, when someone came in needing a new evaporative cooler for their house you didn't have to be a rocket scientist to explain that having cool air when it's really hot is a benefit. There was a period of time where I had changed my major to business, due to my super-sharp retail sales ability. This was totally misguided, and I felt like a failure at the time. When I look back now, I see the leadership lessons that were provided for me on a daily basis.

I worked for two different department managers during my sales career. The two men, Dan and Jake, were very different. Jake was not overly focused on moving up the ladder, while Dan saw being a store or even regional manager in his future. Working for Jake was always fun, and I felt like he truly valued me and considered me a friend, even though I was at least 10 years younger than him. Jake was very good with constructive feedback and wanted to see each of the sales team improve through support and practice. When the sales floor wasn't busy, Jake would take one or two of us to a product and have us practice our sales work with him playing the role of the customer. He was actually coaching us to be better at what we did.

Dan was not a coach. His leadership style can be summed up by his catch phrase, "Go, Go, Go." He was driven by numbers and data. He ranked the department's sales every day by posting each employee's sales totals very publicly. I am sure the goal was to motivate those toward the bottom to be better, but the reality was, sales were driven most by the schedule, meaning what days and times you worked. Work evenings during the week, you'll be on the bottom. Draw Friday through Sunday's day shifts, and you were king of the hill. Dan was only concerned with sales but did nothing, aside from the rank and shame board, to grow his salespeople.

When I left retail to take my first teaching job, I was stunned by how dramatically different my school's leaders were from Dan. Certainly, this was a completely separate profession, but leadership is leadership, right? Working for Betsy was about being part of a team, about being praised for the work being done, and being seen as more than just a body in a classroom. *It is amazing what people will do, the lengths they will go when they know they are valued as human beings who are loved and trusted.* She knew how best to motivate not only teachers but her students as well. See them as individuals, love and support them, be present and visible, and have their backs when things get tough.

As a teacher, I worked hard in my classroom to make sure every student was heard on a daily basis. I knew that, for many of my kids, school was their primary safe place and wanted them to appreciate being in my classroom and with me. The key to making this type of culture exist was knowing my students and allowing them to know me for who I was. Never was the relationship element more important than a fall day in September of 2001.

If you were alive and old enough to have any memory, you'll never forget September 11, 2001. That particular Tuesday started similarly to other days: my wife and I getting ready to go to school (she was the athletic director's secretary at our high school at the time) and getting our daughter ready to attend daycare, which was at our school. We didn't turn the TV on that morning because we were rushing to make our normal monthly staff meeting. After we dropped our daughter at her daycare, we got out of the car in the school's parking lot. We began to hear the buzz that the twin towers had been hit by hijacked airplanes.

Our staff was looking to our principal for leadership, guidance, and honestly, to hear her say it wasn't real. There were bomb threats coming into our school, and it was decided, initially, the entire student body would be gathered in our gymnasium. Looking across the room at the daycare kids (my child) it hit me that the world would never be the same. For the first time in my life, I was scared to be at school.

Later in the morning, we were allowed to return to our classrooms. I'm sure every teacher in the country did the same thing I did, turned on the TV, watched in horrified awe, and provided comfort for students. Students came and went through the day, but a handful of my kids did not want to go anywhere except my classroom. Many years after this happened, I've talked with those students about this, and they've all said the same thing, "Pep, I wanted to be in your classroom because you made me feel safe." Throughout the time I was a classroom teacher, most of my students worked very hard to be their best. It might have been internal motivation, it may have even been from their parents or from some goal they had about their future career, but I know that most worked hard because of the relationships I had built with them.

LEADING WITH A FOCUS ON CULTURE

Leaving the classroom to become an administrator was not an easy decision, nor was moving my family away from what had become our home. But we were excited and felt it was a good time as our daughter, Liz, had just finished Kindergarten. Moving to Wyoming when she was entering first grade worked out great for the whole family.

One day, Liz came home from school so excited! It had clearly been a great day for her and she summarized it this way:
"Mom, dad!!!! I'm a following student!!!!!"

Jess and I were totally confused, but hey, she was six. We played along and shared her enthusiasm. This went on for a couple of days, the same theme each night. **"Mom, dad!!!! I'm a following student!!!!!"** Finally, we had to ask, "What is a following student?" She had no idea. I asked the principal, "What is a following student?" Again, crickets – nothing. The following Monday, Jess was talking with Liz's teacher when it hit her what this elusive *following student* meant. Liz had entered a story in the Young Author's competition and her book (The Big Red Truck) was a winner. When the principal read the winner's names on the PA system, she began by saying, "The following students..." So, all Liz was getting from that was her name was called after hearing *the following students*. She was so excited about this - she didn't know why her name was being called, apparently, she didn't care either. She was just elated to get recognized over the loudspeaker.

I tell this story often, as I think it is a great example of the power of recognition. As well, the excitement a six-year old had about something this simple cannot be lost on us as educators. Everyone likes to be recognized. Some don't want the public recognition and prefer to be acknowledged in more personal settings, but the power of being seen and appreciated is crucial.

WHY ATHLETICS GET IT RIGHT

Returning to the **two questions**, it was clear our school needed to flip the script and stop focusing so much on what people were doing wrong. It was time to start catching them doing the right things! But that was going to require us knowing what the right things were and how we wanted to recognize them. Lucky for us, a formula already existed, and we already had it in our school (and so do you).

As you recall, it was athletics that got me into education. I wanted, most of all, to be a head basketball coach. I was, at best, an average player but had both a love for and knowledge of the game. During my teaching career I was fortunate enough to be a head coach at the high school level in two different sports. I was a head tennis coach and a head basketball coach. I loved coaching, particularly being at practice. Competing on a daily basis to be better than we were the day before was, to me, the ultimate in teaching and learning. It was easy to measure your progress, to differentiate between athletes of differing skill levels, and frequently finding moments to celebrate.

Recently, I was reminded of a story by a former player and student. Brian was one of my favorite kids to coach. He was a hard worker but wasn't the kid who was in the starting line up. He was talented but had more talented players in front of him. He reminded me of a taller version of myself as a player. I coached Brian in both junior high and high school. In the early part of Brian's eighth grade season, our team was playing one of the best teams in the state in their gym. We were also one of the best teams, and this game lived up to the hype. A back and forth game came down to the last minute or two with the game tied. With four seconds left, the other team hit two free throws to put them up by four points. Most likely, the game was over. Brian was one of the many kids I had who loved to shoot three-point shots, so I said, "Brian, go check in and hit a three." The play was designed for us to, hopefully, get fouled and hit a shot, but the other team chose not to play defense (a very good strategy when you're up by four with only a few seconds left). After two passes the ball was in Brian's hands and he drilled the three-point shot. Our bench erupted and mobbed Brian, including me. It was the first three he had hit in a game, and we celebrated like we had won. We didn't, we lost by one. Although it wasn't the end of the season, it was an awesome game, and our team was thrilled to see one of their own hit that shot.

When Brian retold this story to me, I was reminded why we love sports so much. It's all about competing, being teammates, and celebrating each other when things go right. Brian and his teammates are still friends to this day. I'm sure, along with other stories of athletic success, and probably a lot of stories from off the court, they reflect not on losing a game that day but on how we celebrated Brian. By the way, Brian is married to Sarah, who you met in Chapter 1, and now coaches basketball in that same community. I hear from him throughout their season as he shares successes and struggles from his own team.

If you ask about the average American high school, some community members can tell you if the school is *good* or not but usually can't say much more. When you ask about the football team, basketball team, or wrestling team, you will get a lot more information and passion. Why? Not because sports are more important than academics, but because sports teams have it figured out, and have for a long time. Athletes have the letter jackets, pins, medals, locker signs, and helmet stickers. A kid will run through a brick wall to get a sticker on their helmet. The more stickers they have the more big plays or impact they have made on their team. Along with uniforms that kids are proud to wear, sports teams have an innate unity to them.

The single most important thing you can do is continually build positive culture and climate in your school.

CELEBRATION RALLIES
Think about what would happen if academics were given the same type of celebration as athletics? This would also hold true for activities as well. You've all been to a pep rally before, but instead of having one just for your athletic teams at homecoming or before a big game, consider having a rally just to celebrate academic achievement. Recognize and reward the students who are earning great grades (not just all A's either) along with kids who have raised their GPA by .5 or more. What might it look like if we celebrated grades, attendance, ACT/SAT scores, military

appointments and enlistments, and hirings for awesome jobs right out of school the same way my team celebrated Brian hitting a three-pointer? Having held many academic pep rallies, I can tell you they far and away surpass anything done just for sports.

A staple at our school was the academic pep rally. The first academic pep rally you hold, you'll find confusion from your kids and maybe your adults as well. But schools were built for learning, not for football.

Give it a Theme: Having a theme for your rallies will bring even more energy to the event. We decided to have our first academic rally of the year at Halloween. It fell right at the end of the first quarter, and I convinced the principal (I was still the assistant principal at this time) to let the students wear their costumes that day. The kids BROUGHT IT and had so much fun. Yes, FUN! School can and should be fun. Many of our staffulty even came in costumes. Every year, this was one of the most anticipated events of the year. Here are just a few of the themes we've used:

- Superheros
- Price is Right
- Halloween Horror Movies
- Mission Possible
- The Tonight Show w/Jimmy Fallon
- Super Villains
- ZombieLand

Games: Kids are great at this, create games that kids can play and compete against each other. Keep score by grade level. Everyone wants to beat the seniors, but they almost never do.

Spotlight: Put all the students who have hit the targets you've set in the spotlight. Call out or bring to the floor your 4.0's, 3.5's. Even better, bring out the kids who've raised their GPA by .5 or more. They never get the spotlight - make a big deal of them, they deserve it! Get staffulty involved with a teacher flash mob dance, teachers vs. students dance off, or a lip sync contest. And candy, throw candy into the stands. Make t-shirts with the theme and throw those into the crowd. Crank the music, sing along, have your drum-line perform. Just blow the roof off the joint!! Bring the games, bring the themes, and celebrate all the awesome work your students and your staffulty are doing every day.

RTA BARBECUE

At our high school, we called our positive referral cards the Road to Awesome cards. Anyone could nominate anyone else for the Road to Awesome (RTA), they just needed to fill out the form. It might be a teacher nominating a student for doing well on a test, for helping another student, or for just being caught doing it right. Once the forms were turned in by the monthly deadline, all RTA card recipients were given a ticket stub the day before the event.

On the day of the event, the ticket holders came outside by the cafeteria during their lunch and were treated to a full-scale, barbecue feast. Hamburgers, hot dogs, beans, potato salad, chips and sodas or water. I would partner up with a few other staffulty to man the grills. This was a fun opportunity to do something a little different and to just *be* with kids and staffulty. A quick variation on this topic: when the temperature starts to drop, bring the action inside. Chili nachos, hot dogs, or even a sandwich bar is an option to still feed and recognize while the grill stays out of the snow.

MAD PROPS MONDAY

Keeping with the concept of recognizing, rewarding, and reinforcing the right behaviors, the awesome kids of West Grand High School developed Mad Props Monday. Similar to the Road To Awesome cards, this variation of catching them doing it right gives everyone in the school community the opportunity to give a shout out to those who are doing it right. Every Monday during the announcements, the students read all the Mad Props over the PA system, giving the recipients the shout out they deserved.

THE GOLDEN APPLE

Sometimes, the best recognition comes from those with whom you work closely. Traveling trophies, such as the golden apple, allow staffulty members to recognize their peers in a public fashion. It's simple, just get whatever traveling trophy you want. I've used a golden apple, horseshoes, and have even seen a few schools use a bowling pin.

You and your leadership team can choose the first recipient(s) of the trophy and present them in a staffulty meeting or some other public gathering. From there, the staffulty who receive the trophies must bring them back to the next meeting and recognize one of their peers.

My favorite version of this happened at West Grand in the K-8 school. West Grand schools are the Mustangs, Colts, and Buckaroos. The K-8 decided their traveling trophy would be an actual horseshoe on a massive gold chain. If you are a college football fan, think University of Miami's turnover chain. It was a huge hit.

GETTING CUSTODIANS INVOLVED

Similar to the golden apple, this award is a must for elementary school classrooms. Kids are competitive, and usually, so are their teachers. The concept here is to work with your custodian(s) by having them choose the cleanest classroom each week. Students will work very hard to make sure they are cleaning up after themselves, and this gives the custodian buy-in to the work being done on culture and climate. The cleanest classroom gets to have the golden trash can for one week. Then, the golden trash can rotates to the next winner. Other variations of this traveling trophy can be tied to student behavior, cooperation, quiet transitions in the hallway or other areas of focus.

Here you have an opportunity to capitalize on the people in your community who want to help out but aren't necessarily available to come into your school. At West Grand K-8, the traveling trophies for music, PE, and library were made by the spouse of a teacher. His fabrication skills are top notch.

GIVE THEM SPACE
In those early administrative years, students would sit sprawled about on the floor of our halls before school, at lunch, and after school. Many of us at the school felt this was not OK. Fortunately, our gymnasium was remodeled that summer, and we had an enormous amount of wood planks from the old bleachers left over. In a conversation with a few of the maintenance technicians, they brought up the idea of making benches out of the old wood. Within the span of just a year, we had benches lining nearly every open space in our hallways. They looked great and served a much needed function. Even better, they cost very little money since we had most of the supplies.

Our students were very appreciative, but some of the teachers were a bit skeptical. "What if they vandalize them?" they would say. "What if they don't?" was my response. It turned out we had very little if any damage done to the benches, and they are still in excellent shape.

PRIDE IN YOUR SCHOOL
To start with, clean it up! This may not seem like a significant piece of your school's culture and climate, but if you don't have enough pride to keep it looking good, why would anyone else take pride in your building? Early in my administrative career, I would walk the halls at lunch, patrolling the campus to ensure mischief wasn't afoot. We had a rule, among the many rules, that

food wasn't allowed outside of the cafeteria. This was problematic, to say the least. At the time RSHS had well over 1,100 students and a cafeteria with a capacity of 260. Having three lunch periods helped, along with the campus being open, but expecting our kids to not have food or drinks in our hallways was unrealistic. The most common issue was trash being left on the ground in many parts of the campus. We were taking the same approach that many schools still use to this day, which was to outlaw food and drink.

We were looking at the issue all wrong and were trying to fix the symptom rather than treat the root cause. Kids are not messy on purpose. OK, maybe a few but most are not. In fact, the vast majority of kids will do the right thing and make good choices when presented with the option. So, how do you give them the right options? Treat the root cause, Disney style.

Millions of people visit the Disney parks every year. Somehow, even with that high volume of patrons, the parks are amazingly well maintained and extremely clean. In the early years of the original park's opening, Walt Disney became obsessed with ensuring the park would remain in pristine condition. In a casual study, Walt noticed the average patron would hang on to their garbage no further than 30 feet. It is no coincidence that even today the park is meticulous about having trash receptacles equally spaced throughout. And you will find very little if any trash. My school took on this same approach, adding trash cans at roughly the same distance (sometimes, closer). The result was amazing. We didn't have to ban their beverages or snacks, we simply gave them a spot to put their garbage. They weren't perfect, but it was so much better, and the building's appearance improved dramatically.

A COMMON PLACE

The first day of our winter break, the year Aly painted that first quote, was a Friday. Aside from a few custodians and a couple of the secretaries, I had the building to myself. The beginning of a break was always a time to decompress and just breathe, at least for me. This year was no exception. I've said it before, but being a first year building principal is HARD work and I was exhausted.

Somewhere in the middle part of the morning, one of my secretaries came in and, through eyes filled with tears, shared tragic news. That morning, Aly, the student who'd painted our first quote, had died in a single car accident, and another of our students was badly injured in the wreck. Aly was a kid who'd grown up down the street from our house, and her mom worked at our school. Not only that, I was good friends with her mom.

Shortly after the news came, I found myself standing beneath Aly's quote: "One day your life will flash before your eyes, make sure it's worth watching." I was thinking about the summer my wife and I, along with some other district personnel that included Aly's mom, went to a conference in Las Vegas. Aly went along with her mom so our daughter would have someone to hang out with while the rest of us were in sessions. The two of them were about five years apart, but they had a wonderful time finding every possible ice cream vendor on the Vegas strip that summer. I was devastated and in complete shock.

Before I knew it, a few students had made their way into the school and joined me in that front hallway. The further into the day we went, the more students and staffulty began to show up. By dinner time, the hall was filled, and a vigil planned for the space right outside the door. I knew it was important that day for me to be there with my students, my staffulty, but it was hard. I was grieving and in shock. My heart was broken for her family and for our school family.

It was a common place for me, that hallway was really my true office. But sitting on a bench in the hallway that day was both awful and unifying. Tragedy brings people together. That day, I was given an amazing insight into the mind of our kids. Chase, an incredible student leader, sat with me quite a bit that day. He was one of the first kids who showed up at the school in the morning. As the evening began to get quiet and people returned to their homes, Chase put his arm around me and said, "Pep, how are you doing?" Through the tears I said, "Chase, I'm crushed, but I am glad I could be here for all of you." I will never forget what he said in response, "Pep, we all love you and appreciate that, but you should know I wanted to be here for you."

Highway 40 west of Kremmling, CO under
the clouds on a rainy afternoon.

5

Who Do You Really Serve?

*"Everyone who remembers his own
education remembers teachers, not methods
and techniques. The teacher is the heart of
the educational system."*
~ Sidney Hook

I had a conversation with a good friend who was moving from his role as a building principal into a new role at the district level. He is now serving as an assistant superintendent in a different community than the one in which he was a principal. In addition to learning a new community, building new relationships, and navigating a new system, he was faced with a dilemma. He found himself between the superintendent and a group of principals, uncertain how to please both sides. During our conversation, he asked me for some advice. How do I move from being a building principal to being someone who now is supposed to lead a group of principals? How do I help these unique individuals lead their schools, each of which has its own challenges and strengths, while also meeting the goals and directives of my superintendent? This was an interesting line of questioning, and I was drawn to what had made him successful in the first place. I have built quite a good network of leaders from all over the country, but none that had impressed me more as a true servant leader than this man. My answer to his questions came in the form of a question. **Who do you really serve?**

As leaders, it is essential that we revisit this question often. Who do we really serve and how do we best serve them? It might be the quick and easy answer to say we serve our students. While this is accurate, I ask leaders to think a little deeper about this question. If we want to grow and serve our kids, as leaders, the conduit through which we impact kids is our teachers. In fact, if you want to grow and serve your students as a leader, the most important thing you can do is grow and support your teachers. So, again, who is it you really serve?

SOME DISTURBING TRENDS
Each year during my leadership career, I had to hire new staff to replace the ones who left. The typical rate of turnover that I experienced during 15 years of school and district leadership was around 10% annually. In a 2022 study, Forbes cited the national

average for teacher turnover to be roughly 16%. However, they also stated that we could see a spike in teacher turnover that could go as high as 50%. If you are a school leader, this should terrify you. Where will we find the human capital to ensure we have high-quality teachers in every classroom? Where will we find the critical support staff members? How will novice administrators support them when they are so very new to the job?

Research shows that teachers, especially those early in their careers, are leaving the profession at a high rate. The reasons most cited for career changes are:
1. Emotional Exhaustion & Burnout
2. Lack of Support and Resources - Working Conditions
3. Quality of Life - Work/Life Balance
4. Political & Parental Overreach
5. Pay vs. Demands on Their Time

Think about these five primary reasons for teachers leaving our profession. I am drawn to the realization that we, as leaders, have a great deal of control over most of these issues. We may not all be legislators or employees of state departments of education, but we can and do have a say in the work conditions our teachers are facing. It comes back to the question above: Who is it that you really serve?

Most school leaders would answer this question by saying they serve the students. And they would be absolutely correct. Yet, how is it that you serve your students? You are not the person in the classroom every day. You are not the one building lesson plans, looking at individual student data, losing sleep over the home life a student of yours is faced with every night. Sure, you care deeply about your students, but you are not their teacher. You aren't the paraprofessional in the class each day assisting a student with special needs, changing a diaper or feeding tube. So, I will ask again, who is it that you really serve? My answer would be that you serve your staff.

STAFFULTY (STAFF + FACULTY)

I am a culture builder, so I'm passionate about the importance of everyone, not just the teachers. ***No program, curriculum, or initiative will reach its peak benefit without a culture and climate where everyone feels valued and part of something special.*** I placed an equal value on every person working with kids in my schools. To me, the traditional staff and faculty is divisive. It creates a hierarchy and implies that the teachers are more important than a paraprofessional, librarian, bus driver, food service worker, or custodian. A core belief I hold is that we are all in this together, so let's act like it. The person who impacted me, probably, the most as a student was the high school athletic trainer. Was he any less important than my English or Science teacher? Not in my eyes.

GIVING ROOM TO INNOVATE

As a first year teacher I was given keys, a room number and not much else. It was my job to figure out what was important for students to learn in eighth grade science. Yes, we had some type of basic curriculum outline, but Betsy believed in letting her teachers work to their strengths, work together, and focus on growing a whole child. Now, in fairness, I was in the middle of my classroom teaching career when the No Child Left Behind (NCLB) was passed into law (2002). Most legislatures, state departments of education, and district leaders were still not sure what this legislation would mean, let alone a first year teacher. However, being on the edge between life before and during NCLB, I have a unique perspective and can remember a world before high-stakes testing became the norm. It is for that reason I look for teachers who are willing to innovate in their classrooms rather than simply teach to a test.

Teachers today have so many expectations on their plates. Meeting state standards can be challenging for even the very best teachers. We expect our teachers to have and hold high expectations of their students and to deliver engaging lessons on a daily basis. When leaders follow their core beliefs they convey a clear and consistent message to teachers. Trusting teachers to leverage both the art and the science of teaching is one of the finest compliments leaders can pay their teachers. I consider compliance to be the enemy of innovation. When teachers are given the freedom to innovate and to take risks in their classrooms without fear of reprisal, amazing things happen.

There is a refrain in Shakira's song, *Try Everything,* that applies here. The line, "I want to try everything, I want to try even though I could fail." How do busy school leaders best support teachers and other staffulty members who are trying to be innovative in their teaching practice? I would advocate for you to, **Give them Five!**

- Give them Your Ear
- Give them Space
- Give them Time
- Give them Coaching
- Give them Praise

GIVE THEM YOUR EAR

I am one who will just jump into something and be comfortable with building it on the fly. Not everyone is wired this way and might need someone to be a sounding board. Quite often, we believe that leading means having the solutions to every problem that might be brought our way. As a school leader, staffulty will come to you frequently with areas of struggle or ideas they might be considering. Instead of rushing to be the one with the answers, try asking this question first: **What do you want to do?**

I learned this tool working as a principal with assistant principals who were new in their role. It's easy to tell them the answer or what they should do. However, when asked this question, they would pause and think and most likely come to a similar or better solution than what I had in mind.

When teachers are struggling with something or have an idea that might be different from their regular practice, one of the most effective strategies is to hear them out. I know I need someone to bounce ideas off of a lot of the time, so why would it be different for our teachers, our librarian, or a custodian? Listening can be quickly overlooked as a communication skill, but there may not be a more important tool for leaders. Make sure to listen to understand rather than listening simply to respond.

GIVE THEM SPACE

I broke a bone in my right hand when I was in the seventh grade. My hand was in a cast for a little over six weeks, and being right-handed, everything became a challenge for me. I tried to write with the cast, but it proved too difficult. I chose to learn to write left-handed. Anyone who has encountered this or something similar knows that change can be frustrating. The same holds true for anyone trying something new in their classroom or job role. Just like my teachers didn't ask me immediately how the left-handed experiment was progressing, give your innovators the luxury of space. Let them know you support their efforts and are available to them when they need you, but don't smother those who are trying something creative or a variance from the norm. They will let you know how it's going in their own time.

GIVE THEM TIME

Research shows the number of repetitions necessary to master a new skill could range between 1,000 and 3,000. This is true for learning to make a layup, hit a forehand on the tennis court, or hitting a golf ball. It makes sense, then, to carry this forward to learning a new skill or strategy in a classroom. Teachers need time when they are working on new material and moves in the classroom. Expecting change to happen quickly or to be manifested in any form of data while still learning to perfect technique is unrealistic. Patience is one of the best forms of support you can provide to any staffulty working to improve.

GIVE THEM COACHING

Later, I will share much more on the value and importance of coaching. For now, I will say when anyone is working to improve their skill set, having another set of eyes and some honest feedback will make a tremendous impact. Coaching can often be viewed as only for teachers needing an improvement plan. Nothing could be further from the truth. When I was learning to write with my left hand I would watch the few students in my classes who wrote that way. I would pay attention to how they held their pencil, positioned their arm, and how they moved their wrist. It looked dissimilar to how I created the motion of writing with my right hand. I tried to replicate their movements, and eventually, my penmanship and speed improved. Now, having a coach for ambidextrous undertakings might be unnecessary, but providing the third-point perspective, that outside view for teachers can be powerful. Being there when they are working through a new skill to give feedback and to coach them through the process is essential. Sometimes, as a coach you will model, sometimes you'll give feedback, and sometimes you will be a cheerleader. Either way, coaching is important in the process of continual improvement.

GIVE THEM PRAISE

For any innovative practice to happen in schools, leaders must demonstrate their willingness to support the work. When our adults are working hard to try things that are out of the box, they are showing a lot of bravery and vulnerability. For that reason, it is critical they are praised for their efforts. Let me say that again for clarity, *it is critical they are praised for their efforts.* Do not simply praise successful endeavors, shine spotlights on those who tried and are making adjustments to their new practices. When adults know they have the chance to try things that can improve the performance of their students in the classroom, things that may reinvigorate and bring excitement to schools, they will strive to be awesome!

The opposite holds true in an environment where teachers are afraid of punishment or consequences. They will not try new things, and innovation will not happen. It takes a great deal of effort to build a culture where teachers feel secure and comfortable taking risks. At a time in education when many are chasing test scores and working toward uniformity in classrooms, placing trust in staffulty to be creative and to innovate within their own space is a big culture builder!

GROWING STAFFULTY

In order to best grow our students, leaders must grow the adults working closest with the kids. Leaders push every day for teachers to differentiate their lessons, to meet their kids where they are, and to help raise every kid to a standard. Teachers cannot be successful using a one-size-fits-all approach. We would never advocate for a teacher to teach to the middle and be OK with the results. Why would leaders, then, use the same approach to professional learning for teachers?

Think of it another way. My doctor sees approximately 40 patients every day. Each patient comes in for a different ailment or reason that requires his skills and services. If a doctor were to use the same diagnosis and treatment plan for every patient seen in a given day they'd probably be sued for medical malpractice. Could the same be said for professional development for teachers? If we ask every teacher to do the exact same thing and prescribe identical strategies regardless of the content, age group, or ability of their students, we could be guilty of educational malpractice.

Consider growing teachers in a fashion similar to what should be asked of them in the classroom. Personalizing professional development allows teachers to select growth opportunities applicable to their own work and to the needs of their students. Making professional learning about more than just instructional strategies gives staffulty the time to work on lesson plans and prepare for an upcoming week as well as self-care such as reading, walking, or meditation. I'll share more on this topic in Chapter 7.

STAFFULTY LOVE

Leading a school can drive a person to focus, simply, on the work at hand. Ensuring the right curriculum, resources, and supplies are in the hands of educators is important. Building relationships with parents and continually balancing the partnership with them that is so essential to student success takes up a lot of a leader's time. Being available and visible at events and present in the halls to support students shows how much a leader cares and that they *get it*. But making an impact on those closest to the kids, the staffulty, is the essence of leading a school. I have often been asked what I think is the most important thing leaders can do to impact their staffulty. I think the answer is simple, you have to love them. Just like with kids, if they know how much you care about them, they are willing to do nearly anything on your behalf. The most important thing staffulty can do for me is live the vision we have for our district and our schools. I have no doubt that because they know I love them, they will live that vision out loud.

For clarity, don't go running around telling your staff "I love you" just because you read this book. That is not the point. You can show them through your actions. Some best practices for showing staffulty love are shared here.

Starfish For Inspiration: As the story goes, a little girl is on the beach throwing starfish back into the ocean after high tide. A man, jogging by, stops and asks, "What are you doing?" The girl responds by explaining she is throwing the starfish back into the ocean because if she doesn't they will die. The man, noticing the beach littered with starfish, says "You can't possibly make a difference, there are too many." The girl, picking one up and throwing it back says, "I made a difference for that one."

Every day we are given the opportunity to make a difference in the lives of others. They, too, make a difference for us. It is for this reason that I wear a starfish pin every day. I purchase little bookmarks that have the starfish story on them. The bookmarks also have two starfish pins attached. The idea is to give a bookmark to someone who has made a difference for you. They keep one pin and then give the other one to someone who has made a difference in their life.

I have been giving starfish pins away for quite some time. I enjoy seeing the response of others and hearing their stories about people who have inspired them to action. As an example, Jennifer Stuart (2019 West Grand Teacher of the Year) shared this story with me about the power of paying the starfish forward after receiving a starfish of her own.

— — — — — — — —

PAYING IT FORWARD – JENNIFER STUART

A teacher at West Grand School District (WGSD), who grew up in Grand County, was given the starfish award. The teacher that inspired and impacted her had since retired, but she kept the second starfish in her car in hopes she would encounter the retired teacher. The WGSD teacher was out to eat one night when she spotted this special teacher with her husband at the same restaurant. She quickly went to her car to retrieve the starfish and approached their table. Her teacher immediately recognized her, and they shared in a joyful reunion. Fighting back tears, the WGSD teacher took out the starfish and told her teacher that she had been granted the starfish award for inspiring and caring so much about her students. She went on to say that when she was granted this award, she was given a second starfish to give to the person who inspired and impacted her life. She then presented the retired teacher with her second starfish, and told her that it was for her because the lessons this teacher taught extended far beyond the classroom walls. She thanked her for her unconditional love, support, and positive influence. Now, both emotional, they hugged, and the retired teacher thanked her. Through the starfish award, the WGSD teacher was able to recognize that one teacher that she felt so fortunate to have in her educational journey, and for that, she is extremely grateful.

━━ ━━ ━━ ━━ ━━ ━━ ━━ ━━ ━━

Handwritten Notes: My grandpa was an amazing woodworker. As a kid, my house was filled with lamps, boxes, tables, and coin containers. If you could make it out of wood, chances were we had it and it was made by my grandpa in his shop in Afton, WY. I still have many of his creations in my possession, but the one I've always treasured the most is a small box with my name inside the lid. It is a beautiful box and, upon getting my very own classroom, I couldn't wait to have it on my desk. I've kept a variety of things in the box throughout my lifetime, but after finding a handwritten note on a post-it from my principal, Betsy, nothing else has been allowed to share that space. This note from 25+ years earlier still means the world to me and is STILL in the box on my office desk at home!

Over the course of my career as a leader, I have been very intentional in using handwritten notes. Often, when I have something we give to staffulty, I will put the item in the classroom, workspace, or on their desk (not in the mailbox, if possible) with a handwritten note. One year, I had coffee tumblers made for everyone and put them in their spaces with a note. Another time, I gave out lapel pins stating "I Love My School," again, with handwritten notes. The list goes on, but there is one constant. The item may or may not stay in their possession, but I find those handwritten notes taped to their filing cabinet, on their board held up with magnets, or slid behind the plastic of a notebook they use daily. Another simple twist on this is birthday cards. It's one thing to get a birthday card from your boss, but when that card has a personal note and their signature, it means a lot more. Just like with the note I received all those years ago, the handwritten note conveys how much you genuinely care much more than any item you might purchase.

Cafeteria Takeover: Schools are so good at putting together luncheons and potluck meals. If there is an event to celebrate, we bring the food. These are such great ways to get our staffulty together, but they tend to happen over the lunchtime hour. As a result, the amazing folks in nutrition services, food services or whatever term you are using for the cafeteria staff get left out. Here is an idea to give them the recognition they deserve and to honor their work.

Get your leadership team together with the cafeteria director and identify a day on the calendar when your team can take over. Make sure the menu is accommodating for you as well because YOU will be serving lunch that day. I like to shoot for chicken nuggets or corn dog day (let's be honest, you can't screw these up). Make a reservation at a local restaurant for your cafeteria staff, and let them know the night before (or even surprise them). Then, send them out to lunch, and assure them that your team has lunch under control. The students will love seeing you in a different role and your cafeteria staff will be very grateful. Two things to remember here: 1) take lots of pictures and share it on social media, and 2) make sure the restaurant knows you are picking up the tab so your staff isn't buying their own lunch.

SWAG (Stuff We All Get): In a perfect world, I would have loved to give big pay raises and extended amounts of time off to every staffulty member each year. This, however, requires some elements over which I had no control. Add to it, people in education are not simply motivated by money. Looking for every opportunity to share some love doesn't require a lot of money, just a lot of creativity. SWAG is a great example. Swag can be shirts, pins, stickers, pencils. Come on, be real here – educators love stuff!!

Every year, I liked to have a staffulty shirt or two made plus a few other fun things. Twice I have done baseball jerseys (different districts) where staffulty get to choose the number they want on the back. It is a great way to show unity and, depending on your district, a great excuse to wear jeans at work. Stickers with your school's or district's catch phrase, hashtag, or logo are popular with those who like to decorate their laptops, water bottles, or car windows and bumpers.

Teacher of the Year: No, this is not something that is ground breaking or earth shattering. Yet, somehow, I hear from leaders all around the country who are not using this simple form of praise and acknowledgment. An interesting twist on naming a teacher of the year is to have staffulty and/or students provide the nominations. Another way to make this a special celebration of the staffulty is to announce all the nominees at a big public event. West Grand School District holds an annual spring Celebration of Excellence. At this event, students show off examples of their learning, projects, capstones, and their talents. This was a perfect time to shine the spotlight on all nominees, and blow the roof off for the winner.

Once the winner is announced, nominate them for the state teacher of the year. Take them to a conference, really honor them. Put a big plaque outside their classroom door, get their picture on social media and in the papers. You never know how far it will go. The first West Grand teacher of the year, Nellie Thomson, ended up being a finalist for the Colorado Teacher of the Year. The pride the community felt for her was amazing.

LEADING YOUR PEOPLE

Loving your staffulty is more than trinkets and notes. Being human and vulnerable with them, treating them the way you'd want to be treated is not a magic formula; it is simple common decency. If you want to motivate people, to lead people, then begin from a place of love, and they will follow you anywhere.

6

Listen to Your Students

"Titles don't make you a leader,
impact does."
~ Doug Franklin

My first year as the building principal happened to coincide with one of 2011's most powerful and unstoppable forces, Tebowmania! Early that season, the Broncos were struggling with a new head coach and a rather lackluster roster. Fans wanted to see Tebow, their prized first round draft pick from the previous year. With each Kyle Orton incompletion and subsequent loss the pressure grew on head coach John Fox. Eventually, Fox gave the fans, including me, what they wanted – TEBOW as the starting quarterback.

If you watched the NFL at that time, you know Tebow was an average player. In most of his starts, he completed very few passes and often missed wide-open receivers by a wide margin. Yet somehow, week after week, the Broncos would get a break here and there late in the game, find a way to score and make it closer, then the magic happened. Tebowmania was alive, and the Broncos were the most interesting team in America. As a fan, I will admit they were awful but entertaining to watch. After each amazing play, and often on the sidelines, Tebow (a devout Christian) would take a knee and place his forehead on his fist in an iconic pose dubbed "the Tebow."

The Tebow began sweeping the nation and filled social media with photos and videos of adults and kids alike striking the pose. In many schools, administrators began banning the move, calling it a disruption. Not this guy!! I was frequently doing the Tebow in the front hallway with my kids. We even had the entire student body, including me, doing the Tebow late in a basketball game when we needed a free throw to win.

Often, administrators won't have this type of interaction with their students. My question would be why? Why would you not want to be with your kids and have some fun, letting them see you as a human being and not some stuffy dude in a suit? I am guilty of taking myself too seriously at times during my principalship, heck,

I wore a suit nearly every day. But I never stopped having time to be with my kids, to listen to my kids, and to be there for them. The idea of this chapter is just that, being there for kids and activating them as the leaders they are right now!!

YOU NEVER KNOW

I have a few phrases I used frequently without even noticing. Odds are you do as well. It's important that we think about what we say and are intentional with our words. You never know who's listening and when something we say might make a difference.

Joe Sanfelippo has said often that we don't get to choose which interaction people remember us for, so we should be mindful of how we treat every opportunity to be with people. At one point, I was at a regional function for our area school districts. One of my colleagues pulled me aside to introduce me to someone who had taught with him in a different district. The teacher, Mikala, had been a student at my school for just one year, her freshman year, but remembered me for one single interaction during that time. After connecting with her, and her jogging my memory, she told me the story of a low point in her life and the role I had played. A story I didn't recall at the time but will now remember forever.

Due to some family issues, Mikala had a very tough go her freshman year and was angry at the world. The tipping point happened one morning in the hallway when the words of another student sent her over the edge. She jumped in and started a fight with the other student, resulting in one of my assistant principals (AP) and me separating the two. I rarely handled any discipline as the principal, but this particular day only two administrators were in the school. My AP took the older student, I took Mikala. Fights in the hallway were rare by this point, but our consequences were clear: five days of suspension and the police would be issuing a citation. The process could be handled quickly, and if the guy I told you about early in the book, myself as the AP, would have handled this, he would have yelled at Mikala and kicked her out the door. Instead, I calmed her down and made sure she wasn't injured. But, according to Mikala, it was what I said that made the difference. As I left the room I told her something I have said to kids for quite some time. In fact, I say it frequently enough now I don't even notice it: **Make good choices.**

Hearing Mikala tell this story brought tears to my eyes and a big hug for Mikala. She went on to tell me that not only is she a teacher but painted on the wall in her classroom are my words, "make good choices." Again, you never know who's listening or when you'll say something that will impact another life. I'm proud of Mikala and who she's become. I know she's making good choices with her life.

TRUE STUDENT LEADERSHIP

As a junior high school student, I served as the campaign manager for a friend running for student class president. At the time, it seemed really cool and felt really important. The future of our seventh grade class hung in the balance, after all. Well, I must not have been any good at my job because my guy didn't win, and somehow, our class survived under the very capable leadership of someone else.

The role of student council is important in schools. We often don't leverage the actual leadership skills these students have nor do we task our non-student council kids with leadership roles. Our students are capable and ready to be much more than figurehead leaders. They are ready to impact our communities and our schools now, and we must allow them the opportunity to do so.

Students bring ideas to us as leaders quite frequently. If this isn't happening we should be asking ourselves why. Is it possible we shot down a few ideas, and word has spread? Do we have a culture in place that allows for student voice and opportunity to make an impact? Sometimes, these might be smaller ideas, other times, big ideas that have lasting impact. The key is to not say no to student concepts, but to turn them into teachable moments. There are three examples of this below: one is a smaller idea, one is quite large, and one that came simply from knowing the passions of a student.

The first example comes from two middle school students at the West Grand K-8 school. They approached their assistant principal and mentioned that they wished they had access to water bottles more frequently, especially after volleyball practice. The AP asked for a little more information and quickly realized they were asking for a vending machine for their school. This was not something he had dealt with before, so he wasn't sure what to do. Rather than solve the problem for the students, or simply dismiss them, he asked them to put together a proposal for what they were thinking. The students did just that. They performed a simple survey of their student body and pitched their idea to the members of the leadership cabinet, including me. This was an awesome, teachable moment for the two students as they found the need to dive into USDA regulations, district policy, fire codes and the like. While this took them several presentations they ultimately were able to secure the vendor, appropriate beverages, and get the machine in place. It is still there today, and students are grateful to be able to purchase water and a few other drinks during their day. While this might seem like just a vending machine, the powerful element behind it is the students knowing they can bring ideas forward and make a difference in their school because the adults are listening to them.

The second example came from a high school student while I was still at Rock Springs High. During a summer conference for student council, she heard about another school providing food over the weekend for disadvantaged students. Knowing the challenges our community faced with families in poverty, she saw an opportunity to make an impact. I encouraged her to run with the idea, and along with her career academy director's support, it became her senior capstone project. During a tour of our school I was giving for some community leaders, we stopped into the class in which she was presenting the project. Before we left the room, she had commitments of money, in-kind donations, and pledges of support from the community leaders. The project began by supporting one of the elementary schools with backpacks loaded with meals to send home with students for the weekend. Even after her graduation, the project was handed down year after year, and it now supports every elementary school in the community. Talk about impact!!! When we encourage our kids instead of dismissing their ideas, they can and will have tremendous impact.

This final example should say to us all (in flashing neon lights) listen to your students. Not just what they say but what really lights them up. During my first year as a principal I had a student come visit me in the summer asking to bring a speaker she'd heard at a leadership conference to our school. I am never opposed to letting our students hear from others and was curious. Up to that point, I'd never heard of Rachel's Challenge, a program developed by the parents of Rachel Scott, a victim of the Columbine school shooting. It would have been easy to simply say,"'Yes let's do this." Instead, I asked the student to begin putting in the work to bring the program to our school. It took some time, but we were able to have a speaker from Rachel's Challenge at our school for all students and staffulty to experience. It was a powerful experience for our kids and adults. More importantly, for the student, it was a moment when she knew she was heard and given the opportunity to lead in our school and community.

STUDENT VOICE IN DECISION MAKING
When the team began to form at RSHS to address our school culture, we chose to focus on just a few things to fix. We had many options but chose to focus on poor student attendance first.

Looking at our data showed one of the worst attended class periods was third period. As adults, we were perplexed but began throwing ideas behind why this was the case. We had a rather comprehensive list but decided we should talk with students and get their input. We put a team of kids together, by recommendation of their teachers, and asked for their thoughts. We learned a lot from this exercise, including: adults don't have a clue what kids are thinking!!!

At least that's what we felt. Even with all the items on our list behind poor third period attendance, we had completely missed the mark. I honestly can't recall what was on our list, but what wasn't on the list was the top reason for students. ***THEY WERE HUNGRY!!***

Sure, we saw them coming in with their coffee cups but didn't make the connection. So, why not look to provide snacks for our kids in the middle of the morning. It made a big difference in our attendance. It didn't solve the problem, but it took a big step forward for us.

We leveraged the ideas of our kids even more when we began having academic pep rallies. Ideas we had for themes were quickly dismissed by our kids because, well, adults aren't cool. The kids really saved us and our efforts to improve the culture of the school. Imagine what would have happened had we not listened to our kids and given them a voice to make a difference. The effort would have failed, miserably.

Having a student voice in decision making is essential and can be done in a variety of ways. As a principal, I had one student on the community Chamber of Commerce Board of Directors. The student was a voting member, not just figuratively on the board. Working with the chamber director, we would select a student who could serve for a two-year term. As a superintendent, I had two students sitting on the District Accountability Committee, a committee required by state law. In this case, a middle school student and a high school student served in a leadership role and carried the same weight as any parent, administrator, or teacher in the group.

At one point, WGSD went through the process of developing our learner profile. We collected so much data through a variety of activities but none more important than those completed with our students. Once the information was compiled, a group of high school students were tasked with creating prototypes for the profile. They created four very unique concepts which were shared with our staffulty, the accountability committee, the board of education, and the leadership team. A smaller group of students then worked through all the feedback and developed the final draft of our learner profile. The buy-in from the entire community on this document comes simply from the student-driven nature of the project.

STUDENT OWNERSHIP PAYOFF

Students who are connected to their school are much more likely to be successful and graduate on time. It is imperative that leaders do everything possible to connect students to their schools. There is little doubt that increasing the relevance of instruction for students drastically increases their engagement in learning. The same can be said for their connection to their schools.

Relationships are key to connecting kids to their schools. Every student should have at least one adult who takes a genuine interest in them and notices their accomplishments, challenges, and even when they might be gone for a day or two. As the principal, I tried to get to know my students at least on a first name basis. With between 1200 and 1400 students each year during my tenure, plus a fairly high transient population, this wasn't totally feasible. I would try to have at least 75% of their names down by the end of the year. Freshmen were the most difficult to learn unless they were involved in activities early in the year. I mostly learned their names by being in classrooms and at events.

Jeremy was the exception when it came to freshman. He was a tough kid, a kid like so many of us have met. Jeremy was foul-mouthed, disobedient, and had little to no interest in school. He was hard to be around, had very poor hygiene, and yet, somehow, I knew who he was early in the year. That might be from the amount of time he spent in my APs office, which was quite a bit. Every kid needs love at school, some need it more than others. Jeremy desperately needed our love!

I made an intentional effort to build a relationship with Jeremy, starting with simply calling him by his name in the hallway. Just saying hi to him every day was important to me. I had high hopes for Jeremy but was realistic, knowing he had a tough home life. As the year went by, Jeremy progressed from a head nod in the halls to stopping and saying hi. I can't say he made any headway in the classroom but, you know, baby steps. I sat in the front hall with Jeremy late in his freshman year and asked, "Hey what's the plan? Do you see yourself graduating from high school?" Jeremy told me he didn't have any use for school, and once he turned 16, he was out the door. This was hard to hear – clearly just saying hi wasn't going to be enough to move the needle with him.

As we entered his sophomore year, Jeremy was much more open with me (we even had our own handshake) but still made no attempt to pass classes. He had started the year with maybe one credit. I'm not sure how he'd passed a class, but still, he had one. Only 23 to go. I knew Jeremy would turn 16 later in the year and was hoping to turn him around. A few weeks into the year I was looking into student grades and reviewing the F-list. I noticed a name missing from the list, Jeremy. I quickly looked to see if I had missed something, maybe he had transferred out or switched to the alternative school. Nope, there he was on my screen – and he was passing EVERYTHING!

Yeah, you know where this is going – I *had* made a difference! Not really, actually, Jeremy had been caught making a poor decision and landed on probation. If he were to avoid being sent to the boy's school, he had to pass his classes. And he was. He saw success he didn't know he could have at school. I praised him, was extra enthusiastic with the handshake, but Jeremy still intended to drop out. He just had to make it through probation. But for that year, Jeremy was a better student, or good enough to stay under the judge's radar. Jeremy even went to summer school and recovered a credit he'd lost as a freshman.

Junior year came and Jeremy was still getting by, but just barely. He was tired all the time and missed a few days here and there. Sometime early in second semester, I was manning my usual spot in the front hall and realized I hadn't seen Jeremy in quite a few days. I asked my APs if they'd seen him, but they hadn't. The probation agent happened to be in the hall and pulled me aside. Jeremy, she told me, was in jail. It turned out his mom and older brother had been using Jeremy as their drug mule, having him drive the four hour round trip to Salt Lake City a few times per week in the evening. It started to make sense. But this time, it wasn't just Jeremy. His mom and brother were also in jail.

The next day, I saw Jeremy in the front hall and, as the bell rang, he came straight toward me instead of turning right to head to his Science class. "Pep, we need to talk, NOW," Jeremy said. We sat in the front hall where, through his tears, he told me the whole story. He was being asked, as the only juvenile in his case, to testify against his mom and brother. He also had to graduate, on time, in order to avoid jail time himself. He looked at me desperate for advice. I had none to give. Instead, I said the only thing I knew to say, **"Jeremy, I love you and I believe in you - you're going to be OK."**

Jeremy had a hard decision to make, my role was only to try and build a plan, along with his counselor, to help him graduate. He needed a small miracle, but we are educators! Miracles are our specialty, right!?!?!

The beginning of Jeremy's senior year brought a different kid to our school. He was bright-eyed, wore clean clothes, had showered, even his hair was combed. Jeremy was fired up to take on the challenge. He had aced summer school and, with multiple online courses, credit recovery classes, and a full class load, would make it on time to graduation. I was proud of Jeremy, and I let him know every chance I could. Our handshake had been replaced with a bro-hug. He even got recognized in our academic pep rally! The look on his friends' faces was priceless, and he beamed with pride. I teared up as did many others. Two days to go, Jeremy is on track and has only one big assignment left. This last hurdle was a term paper in his English class, but Jeremy assured me as he left school the night it was due that he had it in the bag. "Heck Pep, it's almost done, and it will be in before midnight."

I was in the hallway the next morning just a few minutes into the day when Jeremy came up the stairs. Freshman Jeremy was back – cussing, angry, ready to storm out the door one final time. He calmed down enough to share with me how his paper was not in by midnight, and his teacher had told him, "Too bad, see you in summer school." Jeremy was destroyed; I was flabbergasted. How could this be? He had the thing basically done. Even a mostly completed paper should have been enough to get him across the line. I went and visited with his teacher and asked for her side of the story. Jeremy hadn't turned in the paper until after 4 am and her deadline was midnight. All or nothing. I proceeded to ask the teacher what she knew about Jeremy. She told me he was a troublemaker and had done nothing for her as a freshman or a sophomore so she wasn't surprised by this lack of meeting a deadline.

There are times, as a leader, when we have to balance personalities, right and wrong, adult and student dynamics. I support my teachers and have their backs. Sometimes, though, we are just plain wrong. We all make mistakes, and in this case, the mistake was not even knowing Jeremy's story. I shared his story, all of it. Including the call I had gotten that morning from his probation officer telling me Jeremy's mom had been released from jail the night before and had caused huge problems at Jeremy's foster home. I understood why he might have been a little late with the paper and now, through her tears she did as well. Jeremy got an A on that paper (probably didn't deserve it) and made it to graduation.

We started a tradition a few years before this time in which all seniors wore a white stole around their neck at graduation. Written on the inside of the stole was a message of gratitude from the senior to the person who made a difference in their journey to graduation. Occasionally, a student would ask for two, wanting to give one to mom and one to dad who had, prior to graduation, divorced. I had parents, grandparents, and others who would tell me stories about receiving the stole and how much it meant to them. Every stole has an amazing story, and I have Jeremy's stole.

My wife and I took County Road 50 toward
Fraser in Grand County, CO. We got caught
in a downpour in the Jeep with the tops and
doors off. We were freezing, but had so
much fun.

7

The Instructional Leader's GPS

"Success is no longer related to the volume of tasks you complete but rather the significance of them."
~ Rory Vaden

When the two students stepped into my office, I was curious as to what they might have as their concern. Both of the young ladies were very high-achieving students and were in the first cohort of the Health Occupations Academy. One of the students, Randi, began our meeting by telling me that her teacher wasn't *teaching* her. The other student, Laura, echoed that. I've had a number of different complaints to deal with during my leadership career, but this was a first. We talked further, with me asking a lot of questions. The two girls shared with me that their biology teacher was using case studies frequently and lecturing very little. The girls wanted, and expected, to listen to a lecture, take notes, take a quiz, take a test. This is what they had been conditioned to believe teaching and learning to be. I assured them that their teacher was pushing them to think deeply, to take ownership of their learning, and that, eventually, they would appreciate the instructional model that was happening in our career academies. Many years later, the two girls consider that teacher to be the best one they ever had and credit him with their ability to find success in college, in their professional lives, and to understand how to solve real world problems.

INSTRUCTIONAL LEADERS

I was having a conversation with a colleague, whom I greatly respect. We were discussing the role principals hold as instructional leaders of their schools. My colleague contended that principals are not instructional leaders. At first, I was rather affronted by this statement, I was the instructional leader of my school as a principal. How can he think this way? The further into the conversation we went, I realized he was saying that while principals want to be the instructional leaders of their respective campuses, they cannot. In most cases, this is due to the heavy demand on their time from other areas.

I was genuinely curious if I was the only principal who struggled with balancing time between organizational management and instructional leadership. I investigated that struggle in my dissertation research and found that I was not alone. From my research, which crossed over considerably with my colleague from above, very little of the time used by principals during the day is actually used for instructional leadership. Typically, principals will focus less than 15% of their time on being the leader of the instructional program. Why does that happen? Most principals want to be that leader, yet they are faced with daily challenges that keep them from doing that all important work. Many principals will have their struggles in either organizational management or instructional leadership. However, when we don't focus on being the instructional leader of the school, student performance is what suffers. If you're interested in reading my dissertation, a link can be found on the About the Author page at the end of this book.

Our schools exist for a specific reason – teaching and learning. One of my favorite quotes is from a friend and fellow Renaissance Hall of Fame member, Dr. Steve Woolf. On his daily announcements, during his time as a middle school principal, Steve would say, "Thank you for making our school a place where teachers can teach and students can learn." After all, that is the goal, the purpose, the reason for the existence of schools.

As a building level administrator, I held two different assistant principal roles prior to becoming the principal. The first, as mentioned in the chapter on school culture, was overseeing discipline and attendance. The second role was leading curriculum, instruction, and all special programs for our school. This meant, in a nutshell, if it happened in a classroom and it wasn't discipline or attendance related, it fell in my purview. I was charged with Advanced Placement (AP) programs, career academies, dual and concurrent enrollment (anything connected to our community college), special education, master scheduling, assessment and testing, counseling, professional development, and a myriad other duties. Another way of describing the job would be to say I was the instructional leader of our school.

Being an instructional leader was a big part of why I wanted to be an administrator. Some will say they chose the path to make a bigger impact and connect to more students. Some, if they are honest, made the move because of the larger paycheck involved with being an administrator. I suppose in my case both of those statements would be true. I wasn't motivated primarily by the money, but being able to make a better living for my family was something I will never apologize for doing. I discovered in my discipline and attendance job that I wasn't able to really have any noticeable role in classroom instruction. So, when the chance came my way to take on the curriculum and instruction position, I jumped at the opportunity.

BEING VISIBLE

I have long believed that for school leaders to be effective, they must be where the action is. I learned from Tom, my coach, that putting time on the calendar to be in classrooms and to interact with our students was not enough. Early in my leadership career, another administrator and I would go out and about on Friday afternoons and spend time in the classrooms. Our teachers appreciated us putting in the effort to stop by, but truthfully, it really didn't make much of a difference.

Teachers want and need feedback to improve their craft. This is not just in the form of their annual evaluations. Far too frequently, the annual evaluation will be very scripted and more focused on how to score the individual on the rubric than on actually trying to help an individual grow and improve.

PROVIDING MEANINGFUL FEEDBACK

I wrote earlier about giving teachers five as a coaching strategy for their growth. This must happen for all of our teachers, not just those that might be struggling in a particular area. This is where meaningful feedback is so critical. As a building administrator, I put my walkthroughs on the calendar to ensure I had the time set aside. More importantly, I put the feedback cycles on the calendar so I would have the opportunity to go talk with the teacher who's classroom I had visited. I wanted to be able to sit down with teachers one-on-one and have a conversation with them in person. Each informal walkthrough invariably produced an opportunity to ask questions, typically open-ended, designed to open the feedback loop. I would ask questions such as:

- What intentional strategies were you using during this particular lesson?
- What was something you felt very strongly about in the lesson?
- Were there choices you made during the lesson you'd maybe do differently?
- What is something I should know about this lesson/class/ curriculum that I probably didn't know during the walkthrough?
- What is something you're working on that I can provide feedback on the next time I'm in the room?

As the instructional leader of the school, I knew I had to be willing to sit down and have these conversations with my teachers. The more of these conversations I had, the more confident I was in what I was asking and the impact my leadership could have on teacher efficacy. This carried forward for me as a superintendent, doing much of the same and making time to visit with teachers in those one on one situations.

RELEVANCE, RIGOR, AND RELATIONSHIPS (THE NEW 3 Rs)

As a school, we knew we needed to show improvement with our student outcomes. Year after year, our data was not showing the growth we were hoping for and working toward. Results from the previous year's assessment data were met with the usual resistance and, honestly, excuses. "Our students see no value in the tests, so they don't try," they'd say. "Kids are more than a test score," some would proclaim. While these are very valid arguments, the truth is we weren't always willing to look at ourselves as a possible root cause of the problem. The same was true of my work as a superintendent. Our assessment scores were decent, but they flatlined. We would go up a point or two, maybe go down a point or two, but we were doing very little to move the needle beyond what had always been.

RELEVANCE
While I was principal, our entire school knew we wanted to improve our student engagement in their learning. I hear this often in working with schools and leaders all over the country. Student engagement is critical. It is very difficult for high quality teaching and learning to happen in its absence. Early in my leadership career, we jumped all-in as a district into cooperative learning strategies. Our curriculum director sent dozens upon dozens of teachers to trainings in all corners of the country. The idea was to increase engagement of our students by having new skills added to our teacher's tool boxes. While this was very good training and made a difference for many teachers, the most important element I've observed to impact student engagement is relevance.

Early in my curriculum and instruction AP role, our school made the move to career and college readiness through the use of career pathway programs. The use of career interest surveys over an extended period of time allowed our leadership team to identify specific career pathways in which our students showed a high level of interest. This led us to plan full career academies. By implementing the Health Occupations Academy, we connected with many students who believed they wanted a career in the medical field. Developing the Energy Resource Academy was essential in a community driven by natural resources and the energy industry. The success of these programs, along with a third academy (fire, law, and leadership), which was added later, demonstrated that connecting students to their potential career interests made a significant difference in how students saw the purpose of their learning.

Students were no longer being lectured to about surgeries, the engineering cycle, or what live first responder calls were like. They were living it. Students were in the workspace and learning from mentors working in their field of interest. As teachers we say things to students over and over and it may not stick, but the first time they hear it from someone in their career pathway it becomes important. Driving the relevance of student work by connecting it to chosen career pathways made an incredible impact on the learning environment and outcomes for our students.

RIGOR

There was a point in my school leadership career when one particular teacher had an alarming failure rate in her classroom. We are talking about something like 60% of students earning D's and F's. I can argue the validity of grades, how they can be very subjective or sometimes used to manipulate behaviors, etc. However, in this teacher's case, she wore the high failure rates as a badge of honor. Parents often requested to have their child removed from the class, which was met by the teacher with joy and pride. "Clearly, another one who just can't hack it," she'd say.

I was compelled to have a conversation with her, many actually. The usual retort when discussing the grade distribution in her room was that she had "very high expectations" and that "my class is the most rigorous." She wanted to prove she was the smartest person in the room. Well, here's the truth: NOBODY CARES. As adults, we must be focused on helping students meet our expectations.

Rigor is not about just making a class hard. Rigorous instruction pushes students beyond simply remembering facts and figures and into a space where they apply new learning to solve problems and have taken ownership of what they are expected to learn. Connecting students to topics they find relevant and interesting is helpful. Scaffolding our lessons to enable students to leap from low levels of cognitive demand to much more complex thinking is important. Building students up to believe in their abilities to meet the high expectations associated with true rigor is the science of quality teaching and learning programs.

RELATIONSHIPS

The magic of what I call the new 3 Rs is that when they all come together, incredible teaching and learning are not only possible, they are inevitable. While this can take place in many different settings of learning, I will keep this focused on the career academies. The structure of these programs, essentially, had cohorts of students together for a three year period. Students were learning not only content but important skills they would use in their lives regardless of the career path they would take. Students worked in cooperative groups frequently and made presentations about their learning in a variety of settings, often in front of business partners in their chosen fields. This led to very strong relationships between students and teachers, students and community partners, and within the cohort itself. It became one of the most powerful elements in the entire experience. When combining authentic, relevant learning experiences with well-crafted lessons filled with high expectations of learning and creating an environment where everyone learns collaboratively and leverages their relationships to have the entire group succeed, it was pure magic. The multitude of students finding incredible success in the career pathway programs are testament to the work done by great teachers and leaders who wanted only the best for students. The best beyond a test score, the best for student futures.

POINT OF VIEW – BRUCE METZ

A lot of things have changed in education since I greeted my first class in 1985. Kids are still kids, and for the most part, they are good and really do want to learn. Providing that learning is what has changed over the years. Old pedagogies with new names become the in thing, but the goal has always remained the same – give students a quality education that can take them into the world of work or onto the next step in their educational process. Teachers have always wanted to make learning rigorous and to make the learning in their classrooms meaningful. However, just because the class is rigorous, we can't always say that it is, at the same time, meaningful. To me, a class that is meaningful is a class that shows students relevance. Every teacher has heard the dreaded words, "Why do I need to know this," and "How does this help me?" I certainly did until I realized that rigor and relevance could not occur without developing a learning community within your classroom. You can't teach kids you don't know and, according to Rita Pearson, "Every kid needs a champion." She later goes on to say, in her very famous Ted Talk, "Kids don't learn from people they don't like." It took me many years to really understand how important those words are when trying to create a healthy classroom. One where kids understand the why in the lesson, and one where kids know that expectations are high, and content will be rigorous. However, if teachers spend time building relationships with their students, the rigor and relevance fall right into place. I've always said that the only way to a student's brain is through their heart. They must know that you, as a teacher, care about them, not only in a classroom setting but in an everyday setting. They look to see if you follow their extracurricular activities or not. They need to know that you are available if they need you, maybe not for help with an assignment but help with something more tangible to their lives outside of school. It is very scary for many educators to put themselves out there, but trust me, it is so, so worth it. If these relationships are developed, teachers will find that students don't want to disappoint their teacher. They will work to become part of that very special community that will enable the educational process to flourish within the classroom, and success will certainly become the result.

Schools are constantly struggling with the problem of trying to produce students that, upon graduation, can show proficiency on their state standards and are career ready for whatever occupation they choose to pursue. My school struggled with these very issues. Because of unsatisfactory standardized test scores, low graduation rates, and students that weren't adequately prepared to choose a career after high school, our district decided to adopt a career academy model to address these very important issues. I became the Director of the Health Occupations Career Academy. The academy model is based on the 3 Rs: Rigor, Relevance and Relationships. I had no idea how these three principals would not only affect me as a teaching professional but also the students that desired to become part of this program. Students in the academy were expected to complete various requirements during their three years in the program. These requirements were not randomly selected. Business partners were consulted as to what skills they wanted our students to have upon leaving high school. Some of the skills recommended and implemented were communication and collaboration, job shadowing, soft skills, and above all else, community service. Students were able to shadow professionals in their day-to-day routine from experiencing an emergency patient transfer via road or air ambulance, observing a baby being born and even being part of the Apgar process for the newborn, to being allowed to scrub in for a surgical procedure.

The importance of job shadowing wasn't always about finding a career path that the student might want to follow in their future. Sometimes, the experience convinced them that the career path was not for them. Randi, a student mentioned earlier in this chapter, came into the academy wanting to be a pharmacist. She was an exceptional student, and I was confident that if this is what she wanted to pursue she would surely be successful. On her first shadowing experience as a second-year academy student, she was placed at our community hospital shadowing a pharmacist. After completing her rotation, she confided in me that she no longer wanted to become a pharmacist. She realized it was not what she thought it would be. Randi continued job shadowing throughout her junior and senior year and narrowed her career path by focusing on nursing. Randi went on to college and graduated with a BSN degree and is currently completing her Nurse

Anesthetist degree (CRNA) from Gonzaga University. The experiences these students received by shadowing career professionals provided the relevance that allowed them to proceed into the career that best fit their needs and made them understand that the curriculum that was being delivered in the classroom had relevance. The students would see how the health professionals collaborated before reaching a decision, and those collaboration skills were part of the everyday instruction model used within the academy.

Rigor is not only measured by a hard test or an exorbitant number of notes to copy. It's also critical thinking that leads to intelligent, collaborative decision making. Academy students demonstrate rigor not only by developing these critical thinking skills but also by completing their normal high school curriculum while actively enrolling in Advanced Placement coursework. They also take advantage of the important partnership with our community college by completing numerous college level courses during their high school tenure, with some students completing up to 30 hours of college level credits.

Finally, academy students became a family. They cared for each other. If a student was absent from class, other students would reach out to learn why. If a student was struggling with their Algebra class, there were always those within the academy to reach out to help the struggling student succeed. This family environment reached much further than the classroom. Students in the academy not only developed close and meaningful relationships with their peers but also with their teachers and their community. During my leadership in the academy, my students completed over 42,000 hours of community service of various types within our community, while using these hours to develop capstone service projects as part of their culminating graduation requirement.

How does one really measure the success of this Rigor, Relevance and Relationship model? I reached out to my academy alumni by posting a message on Facebook. I asked them to share their journey since graduating from the Health Academy. Within hours of the post, I had received close to 150 responses from students that had either completed health care programs or are currently pursuing health care careers, while still many had decided to pursue alternate careers completing college and trade programs. This 3 Rs approach is successful not only for students in the classroom but for the community that they will ultimately serve.

— — — — — — — —

PROFESSIONAL DEVELOPMENT

For most of my leadership career, I attended a lot of professional development training related to work teachers would do in classrooms. I worked in a district that spared no expense when it came to our opportunities for learning. There was a point in time when my family asked why I traveled as much as I did. I explained that this was due to being able to visit model schools and programs, attend high-level conferences, and build a great network around the country.

A missing element in the professional development I found challenging was the lack of focus on the expertise we had within the walls of our own schools. So often, the best professional learning can be had through a conversation or observation with another teacher in your own hallway. As a school leader and superintendent, I was always grateful when others in similar roles shared their knowledge. The majority of the time, professional development comes from outside experts and not from the teachers in our schools. I wanted to do something about that!

ED CAMP RS

The Ed Camp model of professional learning is not something new, but for my school building, it was. I knew the high levels of expertise at RSHS; after all, I was in their classrooms. But other teachers in the school never had the chance to observe each other nor did they have the chance to visit outside of their PLC structure. Enter Ed Camp RS. We were allotted a couple of our yearly professional development days to use for site-based PD. My instructional team put together a proposal and were able to use the internal knowledge and experiences of our staffulty to learn together.

The most popular sessions were focused on technology integration and differentiation. Staff shared ways they engaged students, modeled their own novel and book study strategies and helped each other to come away with great ways to check for understanding both in a lesson and at the end of a class period. We did this work multiple times over a two-year period, and some amazing growth and camaraderie was the result. As a builder of school culture, this was one of the most powerful things we had done to allow staff to learn on their own terms. I even observed one group having a very deep discussion led by a math teacher and the band director on pulling the applications of math into music. The way our staffulty saw each other as professionals changed dramatically and positively as a result of the Ed Camp work.

CHOICE-BASED PROFESSIONAL DEVELOPMENT
As a superintendent, I wanted to replicate the Ed Camp RS work in WGSD without forcing it into the space before our team was ready. In discussions with the leadership team, it was decided we would go in a slightly different direction. The idea was to implement choice based professional development days. I was blessed to work with an unbelievably talented instructional coach in that district. Our instructional coach (IC) was essentially the de facto curriculum director for our district and was the natural choice to lead and organize this work.

The process was fairly simple. In a similar way to Ed Camp RS, choice based PD was constructed by surveying teachers to see what they might want to share or learn about on an upcoming day. The IC then built a choice board with blocks of time matching the schedule for the day. Teachers then selected which sessions they wished to attend during the course of the day. Here was the twist. Staffulty could select two of the time slots to choose some self-care options (yoga, go for a walk, workout, etc.) as well as time to simply work in their rooms. It was a big hit and, like Ed Camp, a big culture builder.

FINDING THE TIME

A huge challenge every leader is faced with is having sufficient time to complete all the work. In my dissertation research, time management came up as one of the biggest problems of practice. Early career leaders, in particular, may have a difficult go when faced with having to lead the entire organization. The focus of this chapter is on being the instructional leader of the organization. To do this work, leaders must be intentional in their focus on instructional practices within their school. So, how do leaders find the time to be instructional leaders? How did I do it? Here are a few suggestions:

- Identify your top priorities in instructional leadership. This will help bring a sharp focus to where you place your efforts. Simply saying you want to be an instructional leader doesn't make the work happen. Rather, state how often you are going to be in classrooms providing feedback. Perhaps it's placing the priority on attending and participating in certain PLC groups, curriculum adoptions, assessment or data teams, or other specific areas of instruction.
- Develop a grid for each month and block the time needed to complete your priorities each week as well as the organizational management tasks.
- Schedule time to check in on yourself (see balcony leadership in the next chapter).
- Communicate the priorities with your leadership team, office staff, and teachers. This will help them understand what you are focusing on and how you are working to grow and support them.
- Ask for feedback from your staffulty.

- Tell students and parents what you are doing as well. The more people that know what you are doing, the more intentional you will be with your work.

LISTEN TO YOUR STUDENTS

As an instructional leader, the primary focus is supporting our teachers. Let's face it, the most important work instructional leaders can do is grow their teachers. But this isn't done in a vacuum. If our students are excluded from the conversation, we are doing them a disservice and missing a key element of feedback. I reference my time on the benches often in this book. That was time I cherished for so many reasons. One of those reasons was getting an inside look at what students were seeing in the classroom. If you want to know what is going on in the classroom, just ask a kid, right?

The master schedule is one of the overlooked parts of being the instructional leader in the school. I was responsible for building the master schedule for many years. Most people looked at the big magnet board with all the classes and cringed, but I got excited. Getting feedback on the schedule from my students helped me build the best possible schedule to ensure access to a great variety of our offerings.

COMING FULL CIRCLE

Years of conversations on the benches with students have left me with some amazing memories. One of the most powerful of those happened in my final year as a high school principal. I was blessed to have a student named Pavel, who would be graduating that year. Pavel was a strong student, great student leader, Eagle Scout, and had lofty goals for himself post-high school. It was Pavel's dream to fly fighter jets in the Air Force or Navy. As the year came to an end, Pavel not only received an appointment offer from the Air Force but from the Navy as well. This doesn't happen very often, and he had a tough choice to make. We had visited on the benches about the similarities and differences in the two branches of the services. Finally, he had made his choice.

A week or so after declaring his decision and receiving the appointment at our senior honors night, Pavel sat down with me again on a bench. He said, "Pep, can you talk with me about leadership?" I told him it was one of my favorite topics and asked what he specifically wanted to discuss. He shared his views of the work I led at our school and his appreciation of my leadership. It was for that reason that he wanted my input, my insights into leadership as a career. I asked why, knowing he was bound for greatness as a fighter pilot. "Pep," Pavel said, "I found out during my final physical exam that I have some color blindness. They aren't going to let me fly." I bit my lip, gave him a hug and said, "Tell me why you want to pursue leadership?" Pavel said he had been blessed with great leaders in his life: his dad, scout leader, and me. He was considering a shift into the officer corp program and felt it was a great fit. I told him that I was proud of him and couldn't agree more. When we take the time to listen to our students, spend time with them on the benches, we are rewarded with relationships that last a lifetime.

Highway 40 through Byers Canyon
paralleling the Colorado River outside Hot
Sulphur Springs, CO. This photo was taken
from the top of the canyon which was not far
from our home in Hot Sulphur Springs. This
was always a quick Jeep ride to the top of the
canyon.

8

Leading with a Coaching Mindset

"Each person holds so much power within themselves that needs to be let out. Sometimes they just need a little nudge, a little direction, a little support, a little coaching, and the greatest things can happen."
~ Pete Carroll

The game was tied, 53-53 with just three seconds remaining in overtime. As the ball was tipped out of bounds under our basket, I turned to my assistant coach, Danny, asking if I had a timeout. Calmly he said, "Just run your best inbounds play here." I looked to Tennil (my point guard) and signaled the play. The play was designed for Rachel, who glanced at me with a little smile. As the players began moving and Rachel came off her screen, Tennil hit her in the hands (up high), perfect for a catch and shoot play. As the ball left Rachel's hand, my hands went into the air, celebrating the victory before the ball had even gone through the net. **SWISH!!!** *At the horn, game over! In that moment, Danny was the best coach I could have had - he kept me calm, gave me advice, and helped all of us to be successful.*

Being an assistant principal meant I was not able to continue coaching. So I translated my love of basketball from coaching to being the announcer. The view from the scorer's table is amazing. You are right on the mid-court stripe and in the middle of the action. What I found, though, was I couldn't see every part of the game because I was stationary in my seat. As a coach I was able to move around a little bit so the view was a bit better. Once I became the principal, I gave up the announcer role to be more available during the game. The gym at my high school has a floor level and a balcony level. Standing on the balcony level is an entirely different view from the floor level. I kind of wished I could have coached from that level. It is amazing what you can see when you're on the balcony looking down on the action. I could read defenses so much quicker, could identify patterns in offensive plays as well as small changes in how a player was shooting the ball or seeing the floor.

The same is true in leadership. As leaders we are do-ers. We want to be in the middle of the action and involved in the day to day work, and we should be, right?! But there comes a point when as the leader you have to be able to see the big picture – the view from the balcony, so to speak. As a leader, spending time on the balcony is essential to long term success in the organization. Often, we will have some form of strategic plan or goals for the course of a school year. This equates well to the game plan a coach puts in place for an upcoming match. When the whistle blows, the coach trusts the players to execute the game plan while making some adjustments from the sideline, working to reach the best outcome, a win.

On the bus ride home, I would pop in the game film and be able to see the view from the balcony where our camera was positioned. This wasn't just watching the game; it was focusing on certain aspects that went well or were areas where we struggled. Being a school leader is very similar to being a basketball coach. Actually, it's similar to being a coach of any sport or sponsor of nearly any activity. Yet, as leaders, we often get so caught up in the work that we forget to stop and watch the game film.

BALCONY LEADERSHIP

As a principal, I found myself standing on the balcony of our main gym looking down at the floor at least a few times per month. Not during a game. I'm talking about times when the gym was empty and I could be alone with my thoughts. After I started working with Tom and became clearer about what the work really was, I realized I had to set time aside to actually reflect on my progress. The analogy of the balcony was so strong for me that I could look down at the floor and see in my mind's eye those things I held most important in my role. These balcony sessions were necessary for me to remain clear and intentional with my work. I would ask questions of myself that connected to what I valued and felt was important.

Relationships and Interactions: Was I making the connections I needed to make with my kids in the building? Had I missed out on opportunities to meet new students in my school or to thank someone for something they had done to represent our brand well? Who was I missing when talking with staffulty on their prep time? What relationships did I need to repair? Which ones were going well? What about parents, community, business partners? Who did I need to make sure I checked in with soon?

Systems and Their Connections: What was going well and what was a challenge on the operational side of the house? What successes were we having on the academic side? Were my systems working well together? Was there anything that needed a tune-up?

Pressures: Was there anything pushing on me from above? What pressure was I getting from below? Was I balancing my life and my job (usually, the answer here was an emphatic NO)? Was I able to leverage pressure to impact one of the systems in a positive manner?

Climate and Culture: Was there something I needed to do to keep morale high or to give it a boost? How was everyone feeling, and what was I seeing from them? Were there tough conversations that needed to take place to keep the climate and culture where I wanted it to be? Were we keeping the focus on recognizing, reinforcing, and rewarding the positives or were we drifting back to catching them doing it wrong?

Storytelling: When did we last push out positive information or stories about our school/kids/staffulty? Was there something happening in the community or within our walls I needed to be ahead of or addressing to keep bad information from owning the space?

Instructional Leadership: Was I getting into the classrooms and PLCs as frequently as I wanted to, and was that having an impact on student achievement? Did I schedule the time needed to provide meaningful feedback to staffulty after I had been in their rooms? Was I keeping abreast of the struggles and successes of every classroom teacher in the building?

Team: Was I regularly checking in with my team to make sure they had the support and coaching they needed to be successful? Were we on the same page about everything happening in our school? How were we progressing on the goals we'd written for ourselves as a team? Could I have done more to support the growth of any new team members?

The first time I sat and reflected on the balcony, I got a few odd looks from passersby. My secretary even came and checked on me, asking if I was alright. Marilyn was such a wonderful human being. She was so pivotal in the improvement and growth I made as a leader, and this was just one example. Once she understood what I was doing, she made it a sacred time. I really didn't have to explain it to anyone, because she did. My time on the balcony was never just a few minutes but a series of 30-60 minute reflections. Occasionally, I would take my laptop with me so it looked like I was typing or catching up on email. You never need to justify spending quality time on reflection. A few times students even asked about it, and I shared freely what I was thinking. A powerful bit of vulnerability with kids that goes a long way when they understand how introspective you are about your work.

As with any school year, I would get caught up in the weeds of the work and miss some time on the balcony. Once, while prepping my calendar for the week, I noticed that balcony time had been added to Tuesday that week. I hadn't added it to my calendar and wasn't sure how it got there. During my Monday check in, Marilyn told me she had put it on there, and I needed to make sure I didn't miss it. This happened frequently, with Marilyn even suggesting topics for me to consider. They were always connected to my values and my expectations, never to frivolous or simple tasks. A great lesson there: don't waste balcony time on things that aren't important - focus and reflect on your performance around core values and expectations!

COACHING FOR GROWTH AND SUCCESS

As a leader, your job is to create an environment where growth and success are not just possible but inevitable. The work of a leader isn't just *getting work done*. Sure, that is part of it, but more importantly, leaders need to inspire and instill passion and build people. YES, build people. This cannot happen when every interaction between boss and subordinate is evaluative. For growth to happen, for success to happen, we must embrace the belief that all victories begin with a loss, a failed attempt, or a moment when we couldn't do it – yet.

Raise your hand if you've heard about the Power of Yet. Well, of course you have. After all, the concept of growth mindset is not new. Many schools around the country talk about instilling that growth mindset and building what Angela Duckworth calls "grit." But how do we grow this in adults, and how best can we encourage adults to grow it in kids? I believe it comes first and foremost from modeling. This is where I will pound my fist on the table and argue with anyone that coaching is essential for leaders to grow and be their best.

WHY COACHING ISN'T EMBRACED

There is a rather interesting phenomenon that exists not only in education but across the work spectrum related to leadership. Nearly all leaders have worked their way up through the ranks of various roles to become a principal, superintendent, or whatever the title. This is, usually, a result of hard work, continued education, and a lot of success along the way.

People rise into greater leadership positions as a result of their track record, but success in one role does not predict success in the next. Often, the required knowledge may be there, but the support and on-the-job training necessary for greatness doesn't exist. It is just assumed that because someone is a great bus driver, they will be a great transportation director. Why would someone who is a super teacher not automatically be amazing as the principal? Hint: THE JOBS AREN'T THE SAME!! The skill sets required are not the same. However, when these supports are offered in the form of coaching or mentoring, they may be rejected for fear of appearing weak or unable to perform up to the expectations of others on their own.

The beliefs many carry about coaching are varied and tend toward it being something unnecessary. Some will view coaching as just for people who are new or for struggling team members. Sometimes, it is even viewed as the precursor to being fired, like it is some last-ditch effort to save a bad employee. In one of the districts where I was coaching leaders, the superintendent told me that one of their board members asked why I was being paid to "teach the principal how to do his job." This view of coaching is outdated and does not fit at all with a growth mindset.

Other reasons why coaching may be viewed as either unnecessary or a luxury connect to resources a school or district might have available. These may be time, money, or even the personnel to perform such coaching. Consulting coaches are typically not as expensive as some may believe and can alleviate the personnel and time factors. As well, outside coaches bring no preconceived notions, relationships, or agendas to their role. These independent coaches also have no evaluative role leaving them open to asking questions and not telling principals what to do. Finally, a coach can provide genuine feedback and keep the focus on growth and success.

COACHING LEADERS FOR GROWTH AND SUCCESS

Much like an instructional coach would have a cycle for coaching teachers, a coaching cycle is appropriate for leaders as well. Many varied models exist for these coaching cycles and most of them are outstanding. Yet, for leaders, the model and the turnaround for feedback look a little different. Steps for the leadership coaching cycle for continuous growth are as follows:

STEP 1

Initial Observation: Typically, this is best done in a full day or half-day of shadowing the leader. Asking the leader a lot of questions will help develop clarity of priorities and values. While this is an initial step, it is not replicated in the cycle. Additionally, the coach will have many conversations with teachers, office staff, assistant principals, counselors, students, and others. It is important to establish trust and build a relationship.

STEP 2

Defining and Working on The Work: The purpose of this step is to identify what the leader holds as core values, what they view as the important work, and to help frame what work really matters and is impactful. This is an important step and should be revisited annually.

STEP 3

Leader Self-Assessment and Feedback: In this step, the leader identifies what they see as their strengths, where they need to grow, and what current successes and stressors exist. Combining feedback from the coach's discussions with staffulty and students with the leader's self-assessment further informs the leader and the coach.

STEP 4

Goal Setting: Based on the previous step, the leader should identify two or three goals to focus on for a short cycle (3-6 weeks).

STEP 5

Regular Check-In: The coach and leader schedule a regular time to have either face-to-face or phone/video calls for one hour. This is a time for the leader to share progress toward goals, struggles, and successes since the last visit. These are typically weekly or every other week.

STEP 6

Observation Loop: During the cycle, an in-person observation from the coach, including discussions with staffuly and students, further informs on progress the leader is making toward their goals. This also provides an opportunity for adjustment to goals.

STEP 7

Self-Assessment: In this step, the leader assesses themself on their goal progress, strengths and growth areas, noting changes and improvements. This is a great step for celebrating!

Looping for Continuous Growth: Return to step four.

SEVEN AREAS LEADERS BENEFIT FROM COACHING

When thinking about leadership coaching, it is best to focus on broad categories rather than trying to hone in on every behavior a leader might exhibit on a daily basis. As an early career principal I had a few areas that were really big hurdles for me. Tom, my coach, identified very quickly that I was ineffective with my calendar, unwilling to delegate and trust others, and had very few systems in place that would have improved my work. Each leader is unique in their needs and has different experiences and mentors under which they learned and experienced leadership.

Working from a basis of research, mine as well as the research of others, seven areas all leaders can benefit from coaching are:

1. **Time Management:** Being the leader of an organization, regardless of size, will lead to heavy demands on the leader's time. I was asked by an early career principal once how, as she put it, I "did it all." The answer is simple, I didn't. Early in my career I did feel the need to do it all and to be everything to everyone, but I was not successful. The secret to time management is having clear priorities. Of course, things such as the use of an electronic calendar, cell phone reminders and the like are effective, but if you are not clear on what your priorities are, it is difficult to know what to put on that calendar. Much like knowing your core values will drive the work on which you focus, having priorities in your day to day and throughout your year will help put the important things on the calendar and ensure they get accomplished.

2. **Operational Management:** By no stretch of the imagination are the operational parts of being the leader exciting or going to lead to time in the spotlight. Yet, if leaders do not focus on operational work along with the instructional leadership elements, they might be doomed to failure. To add a little more definition for operational management consider the following:
   - **Budget & Resource Management:** Every school district will do this differently. Leaders may have varied levels of control over their budgetary dollars, but being disconnected from where and how money is aligned with the priorities and values of the leader can lead to miscommunication and a lack of trust from the staffulty being led. Spend the time needed to understand, and build a budget that is meaningful and that others understand and can own. Rather than simply telling teachers they will get the same dollar amount each year, ask what they might need or want to improve their

instruction in the classroom. Build a system by which budgetary dollars can be shared through the school to meet those needs from year to year. This increase in transparency and collaboration will lead to better communication and a feeling of being valued and heard.

- **Schedule:** This might include the day-to-day schedule, master schedule, specials rotations, or even the duty schedule for everyone. If leaders make the assumption that everyone will be where they are expected to be at all times but haven't invested the time to gather understanding and support around the schedules a disaster may be lurking around the next corner.

- **Team Coordination:** Every leader loves to go to meetings, right? No, of course not, but they are part of the role that are often overlooked. I have worked with many leaders who say they don't have regular meetings because they respect their team's time. Truth – I have been one of those people. While I don't encourage any leader to hold meetings for the sake of meetings, when a lack of information is present a vacuum is created. That vacuum is almost exclusively filled with misinformation requiring an excessive amount of time to correct. I agree that if the information can come in an email, then send it in an email. Regular meetings in smaller groups, maybe by department, custodial staff, lead teachers, or with the office staff give the face-to-face time needed to clarify and keep everyone focused on the goals and mission at hand. Every leader needs to experiment with the frequency and structure of these meetings, but it cannot be overlooked how important availability to answering questions and listening is for staff culture.

- **Human Resources:** Hiring and onboarding new employees is a small part of what school leaders do, but when done well it will have a strong impact on the school. Likewise, employee discipline and posting and advertising for positions make a big difference in the culture and success of the organization.

- **Delegation:** This could easily be included in the section on time management. As leaders we tend to believe we can or should be doing it all. If we ask others to do something, even a small task, we are showing that we are weak or incapable of doing the job. Just stop it - that was actually what one of my superintendents once said to me. Don't be ridiculous and think you have to do it all - trust the people around you to do their jobs. Give them the skills, coach them up, and get out of their way.

3. **Instructional Leadership:** Most leaders were teachers prior to stepping into the role of school administrator. Serving a school as the instructional leader seems like an easy thing to do until the first time a new leader takes the reins. While most who take on the school leader role believe a great deal of their time will be spent in this area, we know this to be untrue. Nonetheless, guiding instructional programs, monitoring curriculum and learning environments, driving meaningful professional development, and evaluation of teachers can be consuming and leave leaders feeling lost. Support in the area of instructional leadership may assist leaders in continually leading and living the mission and vision of their schools.

4. **Communication:** Perhaps one of the most important and often missed skills of a leader is communication. Having all the knowledge but not sharing it does not help anyone grow or improve. Many leaders who get labeled as failing or struggling simply don't communicate well with others. This might be by oversight or by unintentional efforts. Some leaders don't hold staff meetings because they don't want to take away from their team's time. This is a valid point, but if you aren't giving them the information they would have gotten in that format, you aren't being supportive. Most teachers will be happy to attend

the meeting if the information is important, time is used wisely, and relevant outcomes are evident. Having a coach to support communication can show leaders where they miss opportunities to share out with those who matter.

5. **Climate and Culture:** When we dive in and go to work it can be easy to overlook the health of our school culture and climate. Going through the course of a school year will wear on just about any person. Taking periodic steps to reinforce appreciation of staffulty and students is quite valuable. This might be dropping handwritten notes on everyone's desk, having a mac-n-cheese cook-off on a professional development day, or handing out surprise ice cream bars at the end of the day to kids and staffulty. A coach can be that voice in your ear reminding you to keep the human beings at the forefront and not just standards, test scores, budgets, and the other things that quickly consume you as the leader.

6. **Specific Feedback:** At different times of a school year as well as different points in our careers, feedback needs to be targeted at specific areas. Most of us can identify our strengths and our areas which need growth. One of the best things about having a coach is getting feedback on the things we're working to improve.

7. **Third-Point Perspective:** What we see is our version of reality. That doesn't, however, mean it is *the* reality. Having a coach to provide their perspective and observations in a variety of situations and avail their experiences can help leaders to make better decisions and to slow down when situations become challenging.

REAL–TIME COACHING IN ACTION

Lunch was less than fifteen minutes away when the counselor knocked on Tim's door. I had been working with Tim in a consulting capacity for a few months and was on his campus that day for some next steps. The counselor informed Tim there had been an accident in the back parking lot, and EMS was on the scene. Grabbing the walkie-talkie, out the door Tim and I went, ready for action.

Tim's campus is unique in that it has a fairly substantial population but only one exit from the student parking lot. That exit is where the accident had taken place. The victim was the parent of one of Tim's students and, while not seriously injured, would have to be transported by EMS (tick, tick, tick). The lunch bell was now less than ten minutes away. Checking with law enforcement it was clear to Tim his entry/exit wouldn't be cleared in time for lunch, but he was able to negotiate one-way exiting traffic. Tim assigned his counselor and campus security for traffic control and turned back to me to fill me in.

My suggestions to Tim were:
- Direct your other counselor to get the student of the parent in the accident ASAP, so they can be notified and not hear second hand.
- Ask the person at your front desk to make an announcement to let students know what is happening so they are patient in the lot.
- Push a message out on social media to make all parents and kids aware and you can control the message.
- Call your superintendent - they need to be aware (Tim ran out so fast he forgot his phone). Radio and ask your AP to call the superintendent.
- Walk casually from car to car as kids are driving out, let them know about the delay, and just visit - check seatbelts, be a dad (actually Tim's daughter was a student there at the time, and we saw her driving out too).

Tim absolutely CRUSHED this communication!! Later, his superintendent complimented him and said it was the single-best communication they'd experienced as a superintendent or as a parent (the superintendent also had a daughter in Tim's school at that time).

In times of crisis there can be no question about the importance of communication. These might be small events, like a medical emergency in the hallway, or a big event that might force a lockdown, shelter in place, or evacuation. Rarely will leaders receive criticism for not sharing something they saw in a classroom. But, leave a gap in communication or lack timeliness around a crisis, and there is blood in the water. Just one simple yet strong example of the power of coaching.

YOUR BOSS AS YOUR COACH

Not everyone is going to have a coach either provided as a district in-house support or as an outside consultant. So, can your boss be your coach? This is a great question and is role specific. When I was provided a coach, the superintendent had never been a principal, or a teacher for that matter. He knew he was limited in being able to support my needs for growth. The other superintendents I worked for had not been high school principals. They could definitely support many of the elements for my growth. For the remaining elements I relied on my network of other principals within the state.

When your boss has been in your role they can provide you some coaching, some support, and will want to see you be successful. One of my favorite parts of being a superintendent was helping my principals and assistant principals grow. I was proud of them when I saw their successes and moments of great leadership. As a principal, I took great pride in growing my assistants and those I'd had as administrative interns. The difficulty that exists for anyone who's the boss (I honestly dislike this term, but it will suffice for this section) is the demands on their time. Being a coach for other leaders, along with their own job responsibilities, can put a strain on their boss' time. However, if the focus is really on growth, being intentional about setting time aside on the calendar for the coaching cycle, even an abbreviated version, will allow this work to happen. Being the boss and being the coach might best be summed up by Bradlee Skinner, a rockstar teacher and leader I was blessed to work with as a building principal.

— — — — — — — —

COACHING: DRIVER'S EDUCATION STYLE
– BRADLEE W. SKINNER

At the start of my Sophomore year of high school, I was able to begin the long-standing right of passage known as Driver's Education. As many new drivers experience, there is that thrill of operating a vehicle, yet at the same time, a feeling of trepidation in knowing what could happen if you mess things up. When I began learning with Darrin Peppard, I had those very same feelings. I was excited to be teaching again and thrilled at the culture and climate of the school. It was truly unlike any educational environment I had ever experienced. However, a great deal of fear still existed within me as I was constantly worried that I might make a mistake. You see, I had some forward-thinking ideas about education earlier in my teaching career, which my educational leaders at the time were not too keen about. This led to criticism of my teaching, questioning of my skill, and doubting my ability to be an effective educator. As a result, I left education. When I returned to the classroom with Darrin Peppard as my principal, I was still worried about trying anything new or implementing my ideas out of fear of being criticized or belittled.

When I first sat behind the wheel of the driver's ed vehicle, I knew I was ready and had the skills and knowledge to do what I needed to do. I was confident yet wary. The instructor reassured me that all would be well. He showed me that even though I was in control of the car, he had a brake pedal on his side of the car that he could operate to stop or slow things down if needed. This gave me the peace of mind I needed. That confidence I had was able to take full presence of my driving, and the wariness I was feeling was taken up by the instructor as I knew he was there to help if things went wrong.

Darrin's leadership style was like unto my driver's ed instructor. He did not do the driving or teaching for me (micromanaging), and he was not a backseat driver, constantly criticizing my performance. He let me implement my ideas without fear. He allowed me to take my classes where I knew they needed to be. And as I tend to do, in my eagerness to help students, I might be trying to do too much, too quickly. In those instances Darrin was there to tap that brake and slow things down to a manageable pace. Knowing that he was beside me but, ultimately, allowing me to drive and navigate my journey gave me the confidence I needed to become the teacher I knew I could be.

━━ ━━ ━━ ━━ ━━ ━━ ━━ ━━

BEING ACCOUNTABLE – TO YOU

In the end, your growth and success are in your hands. You are the person who looks back in the mirror each day. I am a believer in focusing on only what we control. Too often, I hear people complaining about things that happen to them or worrying about things they cannot control. Don't waste your time on those things. Whether you are able to have a coach work with you or you simply start a cycle on your own, get out there on the balcony and take stock. Get back to what you value and think deeply about your progress in those areas. It will make a difference. If you are willing to do that, then you are well on your way to traveling the Road To Awesome!

County Road 1 (Trough Road) outside
Kremmling, CO. This road was a scenic drive
with many species of wildlife such as this
deer who was out for a walk with a few
friends. Mountains goats were also very
prevalent on this drive but we didn't see any
that day.

9

Lead Like a Champion

" Every child deserves a champion, an adult
who will never give up on them, who
understands the power of a connection
and insists they become the
best they can possibly be."
~ Rita Pierson

I was at the game, as I always was for this tournament, when the phone rang. I was fairly certain I knew why. Our girls basketball team had just lost their first round match at the state tournament. It had been one of those games. The girls didn't play well, they struggled to hit shots. The officiating was questionable, or at least our fans thought so. The coach was under some fire and had several unhappy parents. You get the picture.

Answering the phone, I heard the voice of one of my staffulty members who had listened to the game over the radio back at home. It was really awesome that our local radio station broadcast all our home and away games over the airwaves, again showing the passion that town has for its school and its sports. The broadcast announcer, we will call him John, exemplified those characteristics but played jump rope with the line between passion and inappropriateness. During our girl's loss he had gone well over the line, and I was being asked to do something about it.

Earlier in the season, John had invited me to join him for the halftime show on a Friday night. We had a great conversation about some of the great things happening at our school (yes, here is an awesome way to tell your school's story) and about how the season was progressing. John concluded our interview by offering an open invitation to do color commentary any time I wanted. As I saw John leaving the arena after our first round loss, I casually said, "Hey John, put those headphones out for me tomorrow. I'd love to join you."

For the duration of the tournament, which was maybe four games combined for girls and boys, I provided color commentary on the radio. I found John a very different announcer when I was at the table with him. His complaining about officiating, coaching decisions, and disgust when players made mistakes seemed to dissipate. When the tournament ended, several staff and community members texted or called thanking me for being on the radio. I knew it wasn't my riveting basketball insight they appreciated. Sometimes, a leader needs to step up and control the message.

TELL THE STORY

I spent a day with a principal friend at his high school. He was having a difficult time with the perceptions people had of his school. At that time, they were wildly successful in athletics, I mean, wow!! They were in the running for, or winning, the state title in every sport. It was super impressive.

As we walked around on the tour, I was introduced to many teachers, students, and other employees. The principal had told me he needed help moving some of his staff forward and was facing a lot of resistance. I heard some of that but also witnessed some moments of greatness. I was struck with how amazing their JROTC program is both from an enrollment perspective and by the pride the students have in the program. A quick stop in the health occupations classroom uncovered another gem, with students working on phlebotomy certifications and actually sticking needles in visitors and their peers. Other cool things included a student creating a case for their phone with the 3D printer, a student creating artwork in the welding shop, and one of the best math bingo games I've seen. Yet, when we got back to his office, the principal was completely focused on the negativity he was faced with as his big obstacle.

Much like my life before the two questions, he was so focused on what his staff was doing wrong that he could not see all the things they were getting right. And their stories needed to be told.

Leaders have so many different roles they play. The role of the school leader has changed dramatically over the past ten or fifteen years. Among the duties that have evolved most during that time is being the narrator of the story. It is no longer enough to manage people, budgets, and curriculum. School leaders must be the face of their organization and be adept in marketing and communicating the reality of their organizations. George Couros famously said, "We need to make the positive so loud that the negative becomes almost impossible to hear." Your presence on and use of social media, communication, and focus on finding stories that need to be told will keep you in position to be the author of the story.

LEAD FROM THE FRONT

During one of my first years in the principalship, I received a troubling call from the district office. A threat had been made on the national level against schools, and while vague, our schools were included in the potential threat. After gathering the information I needed from our district leaders, I took three deep breaths, set aside the disbelief and fear from what I had just heard, and called my leadership team together. Our district's initial intent was to evacuate our buildings to a different location, from which we would release our students into their parents' care. When my team came together, we had approximately 45 minutes to identify not only our plan but to put it into action. As we began putting the finishing touches on our modified evacuation process, the call came that we would be dismissing our students from the school early that day, rather than transport them all across town. Because of the nature of the threat, in this case, a bomb threat, we needed to ensure we contacted all parents regardless of how students left for the day: driving themselves, riding with a friend, on the bus, etc. There were so many logistical things we had to do to ensure the safety of our students and our staffulty, but with a calm head and a great team, anything can be accomplished. Once our students had been released for the day, I called my staffulty together and told them what was happening. I was so grateful for their ability to respond under pressure and for remaining calm. I informed them they were to leave the building for the day immediately and that I would stay behind with the 15 or so students who were still waiting for their transportation home. Many of my staffulty chose to stay with me, even when we outnumbered the students who still waited. As the last student rode away in their parent's vehicle, one of my staffulty members calmly, but with tears in her eyes, thanked me for my leadership that day. While I appreciated that, it was her next statement that left an impact on me forever. She simply asked me, "Darrin, how are you holding up?" I smiled and said, "I'm OK, a bit freaked out, but OK." She gave me a hug, and I began to sob, nearly uncontrollably. I knew our kids and our staffulty were out of danger and felt safe with this person. But the truth is, I'd been quite scared facing down a threat I'd never dealt with before. We never know how we will react to intense situations until the time comes and the pressure is on. On this particular day, my instincts told me to protect those around me, to remain focused on what needed to get done, and to set the fear aside.

As a leader, remaining calm at the center of chaos is the best way to help others in difficult situations. If the leader can't remain calm then nobody will remain calm. Sometimes, the best leaders will be the champion of their organization by leading from the front.

LEAD FROM THE MIDDLE
As a superintendent in a small district, I was able to do more as an instructional leader than many of my large district counterparts. In the latter part of my first year, there was a clear need for increasing student voice for kids at all levels. After many discussions and conversations with teachers, students, and even my board members, I shared the concept of project-based learning (PBL) with my leadership team. I was curious if we could potentially take this student-voice rich methodology and apply it to our district, Kindergarten through 12th grade. The leadership team was in favor of the work but wanted to know more from the

teachers of our schools. We began having more focused conversations with staffulty and, ultimately, assembled a team of leaders and teachers to visit several PBL schools in California. The team had multiple members from elementary, middle, and high school, along with the high school counselor, to ensure more voices in the decision-making process. The three-day visit was a fact-finding mission with an additional goal on my part of gaining support and momentum for something I believed would be a catalyst for powerful change in the district.

While these types of trips are not uncommon, many superintendents may delegate this trip to someone like the curriculum director or a principal team. I did not delegate the trip; I was right in the middle of it. This wasn't the first time I had been a part of this type of work, but it was my first time doing it as a superintendent. During the visit, I asked as many questions of the host school's teachers and students, as my team. When we show genuine curiosity alongside our team we become part of the team, not just the person leading the team. I could have stayed behind. I could have stayed quiet on the trip, but I chose to dive right in and be a part of the team and the work, which put me squarely leading from the middle.

LEAD FROM THE BACK

Every high school has a mascot, a logo, school colors, and a fight song. Rock Springs High School was no different. We were the Tigers – orange and black! But that was where the consistency in our organization stopped. We had easily 15 different tiger logos being used, a team that added a gray uniform with a slang version of our community name (boy, the superintendent wasn't happy about that one), it was anything but unified. One of the best hires I ever made was naming Thomas Jassman as my activities director (actually, I hired him for a different role then moved him to this one.) Tom and I had a conversation at a point about how much variety we had with our brand identity. He came to me with an idea, and I let him run with it.

For the remainder of that year, Tom led the coaches and activity sponsors through a process to identify one logo, a consistent set of colors (specific to the color code), and a detailed system for ordering new uniforms, spirit gear, and the like. Tom also worked with the booster club to make certain our brand was consistent no matter what. I knew where I wanted this work to go. I didn't have a specific logo in mind, nor did I feel it was my place to choose. I had great trust in Tom and allowed him to lead the process in a way he felt best. He knew I had his back, believed in his work, and as a result, so did his coaches and sponsors. The logo, colors, and way in which they represented the brand was brilliant. I would, occasionally, stop by the meetings to let Tom know I was with him, but this was a great opportunity for me to lead from the back. Honestly, it turned out the best it possibly could have, better than if I'd led it myself.

LEADERS EAT LAST

In his book *Leaders Eat Last: Why Some Teams Pull Together and Others Don't*, Simon Sinek discussed the premise behind leaders eating last. The story here, taken from a military perspective, is that leaders must ensure that those around them are properly cared for, whether that be eating a meal, leading the evacuation during a bomb threat, or any other situation. The best leaders will be those that are able to move into and out of situations knowing when to lead from the front, the middle, or the back. This is the type of leadership that comes with time, repetitions, and developing a clear sense of who you are as a leader.

I have mentioned the importance of clarity and intentionality throughout the course of this book, and in no place is it more important than knowing when, how, and from where to lead. I have shared so many different experiences, thoughts, passions, and beliefs around school leadership. I have talked about culture, staffulty, kids, instructional leadership, and the importance of coaching in this manuscript. So much of this work, when you really boil it down, is work that you can learn or be coached to do well. Being the champion of your organization, on the other hand, is not easily quantified, it's difficult to teach and is very specific and unique to each school leader.

BEING THE CHAMPION OF YOUR SCHOOL

Rita Pierson's quote about every child needing a champion is just as valid for the adults, community members, and anyone else associated with our campuses. In short, every school deserves to have a champion who will tout the strengths, understand the shortcomings, push for greatness, and tell the whole story of the school. The best leaders are going to be *that* champion for their school.

How do you become the champion of your school? For me, it began by building relationships with staffulty, students, parents, and the community. I honestly felt like and was treated like an outsider when I first moved to the community where I ultimately became principal. It takes time, but invest in the relationships, and they will pay off. Being the champion of your organization takes time and cannot be done by simply flipping a switch. New leaders need to understand the investment of time required to become the champion the school needs. It is also important to know that being the champion doesn't mean you are the unquestioned leader. The willingness to be open to suggestions, to understand any criticism lobbed your way, is an essential part of being one of the best leaders.

When you're the champion of the organization, you'll stand up to criticism and take it on, deflecting it from your team. When you're the champion, you'll lead the cheers just as much as you lead the efforts to continually improve the performance of staffulty and students. When you're the champion of your organization you'll understand that you will have to wear many hats and be many different things to different people.

Build Culture Like Phil Jackson: This legendary coach of the Chicago Bulls and Los Angeles Lakers won 10 NBA championships. While he had all-time great players (Michael Jordan, Scottie Pippen, Kobe Bryant, and Shaquille O'Neill), he also had a culture built for winning. In both places, there were many different players that were part of the teams. The culture was such that everyone who came on board knew the expectations and the values, and they were clear about how the work would get accomplished. Champions build a culture that brings everyone into the fold and allows them each to feel heard, seen, valued, and trusted.

Love Like a Parent: A parent's love is different from any other type of love. Parents love you no matter what you do. They help you grow, nurture you, and support you on your journey to being an adult. A champion who loves like a parent seizes every opportunity to grow those around them, pushing them to be their very best. Parents understand when mistakes happen and that they are best used as opportunities to learn. Parents are filled with compassion but know that tough love is sometimes the best course of action, holding us accountable for the decisions and choices we make. Loving students and staffulty unconditionally and never giving up on them is the work of a champion.

Mentor Like Barbara Walters: During her trailblazing career, Barbara Walters was known as a fierce journalist, taking on some of the greatest public and political figures. But that's not the whole story. Walters is credited with mentoring and paving the way for hundreds of female journalists including Oprah Winfrey, Katie Couric, Leslie Stahl, Jane Pauley, Kathie Lee Gifford, and Joy Behar just to name a few. The creator of *The View* was said to have been most proud of her impact on the lives of other female journalists. Champions leave a legacy in those they mentor.

Defend Like Volodymyr Zelenskyy: At the beginning of the Ukrainian war with Russia, Zelenskyy stated "We will not give up anything and will fight for every meter of our land, for every person." His relentless tenacity and passion to defend his homeland galvanized his nation and much of the world in support of the Ukrainian people. Champions find a way, a rally point, to bring everyone together and will defend them with everything they have in them.

Each of these individuals excel in the areas listed but may well struggle in other parts of leadership. The key to being the champion of your school is to know your strengths and lean heavily into them. As a high school principal, I was the champion of my school primarily through building a culture and climate where everyone felt seen, heard, valued, and trusted. I knew I had strengths and limitations. I was smart in constructing the team around me so that others could be the champion in areas where I was less proficient. The best leaders are the champions of their organization by leveraging their strengths and the strengths of others around them. They will lead from the front, the middle, and the back depending on the need, the situation, and skills of those around them. The key is to gain clarity around your strengths, then be very intentional about leading from those strengths. That's what it means to be the champion of your organization.

Me and my Jeep on White Mountain in Rock Springs, WY with Pilot Butte in the background. White Mountain has two-track road all over the top and was a favorite place for my wife and I to take a break from everyday life.

Conclusion

*"If you want to be awesome, you have to
kick all the negative and boring people
out of your life, and arm yourself
with awesomeness imbued with
positivity, creativity and a little
bit of craziness."*
~ Rajdeep Sarkar

Traveling the road to awesome has become a way of life for me. I know whatever destination lies ahead for me, it will truly be AWESOME. It wasn't always like that though. I believed happiness was about chasing the next job up the ladder. I had to prove I could out work anyone else in my space, be the first one in and the last one out of the parking lot. I have been part of, and even led, schools where that competition was encouraged and rewarded. Over the past couple of years, I have discovered that traveling the road to awesome is not about that definition of success. Instead, it is about being driven to get everything out of life that we can. After all, we only get to do this once.

The two questions that split my road in two and sent me on my own pursuit of awesome are unique to me. But the road to awesome is not mine to own. It is mine to share, to be a navigator, and to pick up as many hitchhikers as possible. We all own our journey, and will meet incredible people along the way. Each time the road divides we are given a choice. We can choose how we wish to show up at that point. We can choose to be positive, to look at challenges as opportunities, or we can choose the easy path. Caution: that path is filled with things like blame and negativity. Toxic culture is the order of the day on that road. You might find lots of company on that superhighway, but few of them will be there to support you.

Traveling the road to awesome means being a leader. It means pursuing what we want most in our lives and for our students. But be advised, travelers on the road to awesome may experience exhaustion, empathy fatigue, and burnout. When we pour ourselves into others repeatedly, we might drain our reserves unless we are intentional about keeping the focus on our own physical, mental, and emotional health. Burnout is a real thing. It isn't a euphemism for being tired. Burnout is physical and emotional exhaustion mixed with a reduction in our own sense of accomplishment or identity. But let me tell you this about burnout: *You cannot be burned out if you were never on fire*

By this, I mean the feeling of burnout comes from emptying all we have into what we do and how we identify ourselves as human beings. The key to overcoming burnout on the road to awesome is finding what it was that lit that fire in the first place and recapturing the magic. We must refuel with whatever ignited the fire. I've felt it. I've experienced burnout, but I have fanned the flames of my passion for culture, climate, and leadership development. I am a teacher at heart and always will be - I've just shifted my classroom into a much bigger space.

Anyone is welcome on the road to awesome. The journey is yours and yours alone, but know that these three core beliefs are shared by all who venture down this path.

1. **Focus on the things you can control, let go of the things you cannot.** There is very little we can actually control in our lives. Controlling how I choose to show up each day is one of them. When my feet hit the floor, I get to decide what energy I will bring to the world and to the people I will encounter. When I let go of the things I cannot control, I am able to see blame and toxic responses in a new light. I realize that instead of pointing the finger at others, I can control how I respond to a challenge or setback. This doesn't mean I show up with blind positivity. Instead, it means I am willing to check myself and my attitude, knowing what I will need to be focused and helpful throughout my day. It means I will act as a thermostat rather than as a thermometer – when presented with a problem, I will work to solve it rather than simply complain about it. It is a choice – choose wisely.

2. **We rise by lifting others.** The more support, kindness, and care we can provide to others, the more that comes back to us tenfold. There are plenty of people in the world who'd rather

step over someone than help them up. On the road to awesome, we reach our hand down, lift others up, and rise as a result.

3. **We change the world, one conversation at a time.** I said it early in the book, and I'll repeat it louder for those in the back – we are in the PEOPLE business. As leaders, it is not about content, industry, or other expertise – it is all about people. You work with, grow, influence, and support people through the power of conversation. I've had so many incredible conversations through the course of my career. Many have affected my choices as forks in the road have appeared. I'd like to think many of those conversations have had similar effects on the other people involved as well. Travelers of the road to awesome: never forget that we change the world, one conversation at a time.

My final thoughts for you, fellow travelers, are these:
- Take the time to gain clarity on what matters to you and what you expect.
- Be intentional with your actions, time, words, and behaviors.
- Set time aside to get on the balcony and check in on yourself.
- Never forget you're in the people business.
- Live the Road to Awesome core values out loud.

When two roads diverge on your journey, take the Road to Awesome and don't look back.

Early spring one year, my wife and I decided to take a drive up on White Mountain in Rock Springs, WY. The road was technically open, but the snow and ice had yet to melt all the way. We didn't make it all the way across the mountain, but we got the Jeep real dirty and had a blast!

Acknowledgements

To acknowledge someone is to recognize them, to legitimize the impact they have had on a project or on your life. A significant portion of my belief set as it pertains to leadership is to recognize, reward, and reinforce behaviors and attitudes we see along the way. There are so many people I'd like to acknowledge and thank for their contributions to not only this work but to my life and career. The unfortunate part of writing this portion of the book is you inevitably leave someone out, which is definitely not my intention.

To Sarah Brady, Eric Lillis, Bruce Metz, and Bradlee W. Skinner: thank you for your contributions to this book. Each of your stories are important and align with the Road to Awesome message. More importantly, you have all had an incredible impact on me. I love you all.

A lot of work went into revising this book and creating the second edition. It may not seem overly complicated, but many conversations took place around the updates and the two new chapters to ensure quality content. Likewise, working to capture the journey itself required a lot of time looking at photos and, in the case of Kingman, making a return trip to capture the essence of Route 66. Thank you to Eric Lillis, Matt Ladendecker, and Bill Schleeter for spending the day with us and allowing some great pictures with the '69 Chevelle and the '21 Corvette to be taken on old 66. Seriously folks, riding in the Corvette was worth the trip all by itself.

To the people who have pushed me, believed in my work, and taken a chance on me, THANK YOU! To the entire Road to Awesome family of authors, contributors, and fans – you are why I do what I do, and I am forever grateful to you.

To my parents and my sisters: unconditional love is exactly what it says it is, and I appreciate all the undying support from you all. I would not be on this amazing road without the four of you.

To my wife, Jessica, and daughter, Liz, thank you for being with me on this amazing ride. If there is something beyond unconditional love, it is what we have for each other. I could go on and on about the two of you, and our two amazing dogs, but know that I love you with all my heart and cannot imagine this journey without you.

Darrin Peppard, Matt Ladendecker, and Eric Lillis
next to Matt's 2021 Corvette
on Route 66 in Kingman, AZ

Bill Schleeter in his 1969 GTO
on Route 66 on the way to Oatman, AZ

About the Author

Dr. Darrin Peppard is a recovering high school principal, leadership coach, consultant, and speaker focused on organizational culture and climate, and coaching emerging leaders. Darrin is a best-selling author and is the host of the Leaning into Leadership podcast. He spent 26 years in public education, serving as a middle and high school teacher and coach in Kingman, Arizona for 11 years. He was then a high school assistant principal and principal in Rock Springs, Wyoming for 11 years. Darrin's final four years in public education were as the Superintendent of Schools in West Grand School District in Colorado. He was named the 2015 Jostens Renaissance National Educator of the Year and was the 2016 Wyoming Secondary School Principal of the Year. In 2019, Darrin was inducted into the Jostens Renaissance Educator Hall of Fame.

Darrin's work now focuses on supporting emerging leaders and sharing the Road to Awesome message of culture, climate, and leadership. He is the lead innovator of Road to Awesome, LLC which provides coaching and consulting for leaders, inspirational keynote speeches for leaders of all walks of life, and publishes books by educators for educators.

Darrin and his wife, Jessica, daughter, Liz, and two dogs, Phoenix and Dexter, currently live in Omaha, Nebraska. Darrin is a passionate but lousy golfer and enjoys time with family and in his Jeep.

Link to Darrin's dissertation:

Bring Darrin to Your School or Event

Darrin is an award-winning expert in school leadership as well as *THE* innovator of Road to Awesome school culture and climate. Darrin will tailor his work to meet your school's or district's challenges. Darrin will navigate you through the most important pieces of leadership to get your school on the Road To Awesome!

SPEAKING TOPICS
Road to Awesome
- Take leaders on a deep-dive into their core values
- Detail successful strategies for game-changing school leadership
- Ignite a fire in leaders of all experience levels and challenge their thinking
- Get your leadership on the Road To Awesome

Game Changers
- How to **lead** your school with a culture focused on **relationships, academics, and excellence**
- How to make the **look of your school personalized and give students prid**e in their campus
- How to give **meaningful recognition** to adults and students to ensure they feel valued and part of their school's culture

High Performance Leadership Teams
- A focus on 5 keys to building an awesome leadership team
  - Clarity of value, mission, and goals
  - Knowing the house (strengths, fit, leveraging each other)

- Getting work done (workflow and sandboxes)
- Team dynamics (trust, delegation, and communication)
- Continuous evolution (celebration, learning, growing)

The Power of an Educator

- A powerful reminder of the impact educators have on their communities
- Sharing our stories is crucial – Darrin pushes his audience in this workshop or keynote to find their own powerful narratives and to share them with each other
- Nobody is "just a" in this session, Darrin ignites the fire in all staff including aides, secretaries, bus drivers, and more to remember they have an opportunity to have a significant impact on the life of a child.

Connect with Darrin on Social Media
Twitter: DarrinMPeppard
Instagram: darrin_m_peppard
Facebook: Darrin M Peppard
LinkedIn: Darrin M Peppard EdD
YouTube: Darrin M Peppard EdD

Email Darrin
darrin@roadtoawesome.net

Website:
www.roadtoawesome.net

More Books from Road to Awesome

Taking the Leap: A Field Guide for Aspiring School Leaders by
Robert F. Breyer

TRANSFORM: Techy Notes to Make Learning Sticky
by Debbie Tannenbaum

Becoming Principal: A Leadership Journey & The Story of School
Community by Dr. Jeff Prickett

Elevate Your Vibe: Action Planning with Purpose
by Lisa Toebben

#OwnYourEpic: Leadership Lessons in Owning Your Voice and
Your Story by Dr. Jay Dostal

The Design Thinking, Entrepreneurial, Visionary Planning Leader:
A Practical Guide for Thriving in Ambiguity
by Dr. Michael Nagler

Becoming the Change: Five Essential Elements to Being
Your Best Self by Dan Wolfe

inspired: moments that matter
by Melissa Wright

Foundations of Instructional Coaching: Impact People, Improve
Instruction, Increase Success by Ashley Hubner

Out of the Trenches: Stories of Resilient Educators
by Dana Goodier

Principled Leader
by Bobby Pollicino

Children's Books from Road to Awesome

Road to Awesome A Journey for Kids
by Jillian DuBois and Darrin M. Peppard

Emersyn Blake and the Spotted Salamander
by Kim Collazo

Theodore Edward Makes a New Friend
by Alyssa Schmidt

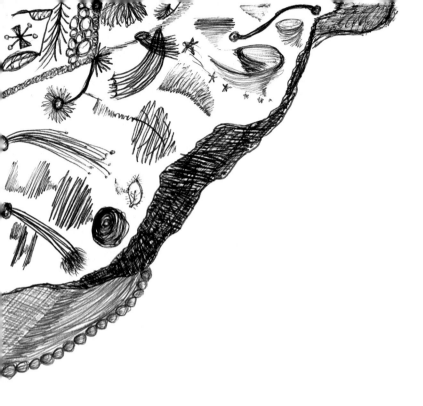

Made in the USA
Middletown, DE
06 February 2023

24041580R00096